Sell More Products, More Profitably, More Often

Sell More Products, More Profitably, More Often

—

ISBN: 1507544367
ISBN 13: 9781507544365

Contents

Hello

In a triathlon, the winning triathlete is the person who completes the event before all other competitors. To do this, they work on all aspects of their race. For example, they may consider their technique in sprinting to the water's edge, their approach when swimming through ocean waves, the way they cycle within a group of competitors, how they run in a measured manner and how they sprint at the race end. They might also work on their upper body strength, their core strength, their mindset and many other factors.

To win the race they don't need to be the best swimmer, cyclist or runner in the field. They simply need to be the first one to complete the race. In other words, they need to be the best at *combining* all of the disciplines required.

What does this have to do with sales?

In direct business-to-business sales the same concept applies. In this book we address the many attributes, skills and disciplines you may require to become the best sales person in your field, the best in your market. (Obviously it's possible to further develop skills on all of the topics we discuss, but to spend time doing this won't necessarily take us closer to our main aim).

To be the best sales person in your market you don't need to have the best goal-setting technique, or the best understanding of communication and linguistics. That's because achieving excellence in an individual skill doesn't necessarily deliver us to our prime objective of being the best sales person in our field, i.e. winning the 'triathlon'.

Let's cut to the chase

Our approach to sales education has been extensively developed, but we like to keep things simple. We deliver digestible chunks of information, dispensing with theoretical rhetoric and academia. We cut to the chase and tell you how it is, without wasting your precious time. We concentrate on what the sales person should be thinking when they're out in the field meeting with a potential customer.

We invite you to become immersed, recall what you once did or try something you may not have thought of. Question your actions. Question your thought process and your use of time. Personalize our comments and selling suggestions in order to improve your sales performance and achieve more. Then return to the book as your perspective grows and changes, as what may once have seemed academic, may now appear excitingly relevant.

We encourage you to think, plan, arrange and organize your future achievements and prepare for action, for all-conquering action. And then act. Act enthusiastically, joyously, emphatically, positively in a focused, determined and committed way towards your sales success. And in turn, to your personal goals.

Our aim is clear. We want to help you sell more products, more profitably, more often.

We know that success in direct sales is all about you – *how* you sell, not *what* you sell.

In fact, we believe that a great sales person with an inferior product will always outperform a poor sales person with a superior product.

Products and solutions come and go, and they all have benefits and disadvantages – the difference in selling them is always YOU. How well you craft your sales story, how well you listen, how prepared you are for meetings and how professionally you present yourself, are all factors you can control.

Profit from our knowledge

Successful business is profitable business. And profitable business starts with selling more products, more profitably and more often. The art of selling and having sales skills that enable you to sell at higher price points than your competitors, or your colleagues, is the ultimate prestige in our profession.

Your business title is not relevant (because there are many), but we specifically address sales people and business owners who are selling products to business customers.

Quite deliberately, we have a commercial mindset toward selling. Our commercial mindset deals with the reality that:

- In our world you don't get "something for nothing."
- You should be accountable for your own actions.
- You need to work if you want to be successful and profitable.
- There is no such thing as instant success.

If the following comments resonate with you:

"I would sell more if we had the range of products our competitors do."
"We had to go in very tight because of the competition and the size of the deal."
"We just don't have the brand or market presence that we need."

Then we especially welcome you to *Sell more products, more profitably, more often.*

We believe in the power of one. And when you read this book, so will you.

One final thing

Because we believe strongly in keeping things simple, whenever we refer to a "customer" in this book, we use this term to cover either a potential customer or prospect, or an existing customer.

In the same way, when we use the word, "product" or "products" we use the term to cover any or all of the products, services or solutions that are being sold across industries, including yours.

Stories from the front line

Selling red apples

The problem

Mario sold apples at the local provincial market. The market was open Thursday through to Sunday. His little 6' x 6' apple stall had always done well for him. The first six years were fantastic; business was profitable, consistent and easy. But times had changed.

Over the past two years, competition had stifled profits. Where he once had few competitors, now everyone around him seemed to sell apples. The other sole traders had all sold out to larger operators in the market so now he was the only stall that didn't offer a range of fruits and vegetables. In fact, he was the only single product stall left in the market!

Prices had become particularly keen since Mr. and Mrs. Watson bought the stall next to him. They had the same wholesale supplier and were buying their produce at the same price, but Mario had to lower his price just to compete. Mr. and Mrs. Watson were lovely people, but they seemed to be happy with a much smaller profit margin.

A multinational hyper mart opened across the road from the market entrance, a mere hundred yards from Mario's stall. The hyper mart sold their apples at prices Mario could not even buy his local produce for. To make matters worse, a twenty four hour convenience store, offering an impressive range of fruit, had also opened right next door to the market. To cap it off, Mario's rental costs had significantly increased since property developers had been trying to buy the market from the owner to build luxury condominiums.

The last six months were a struggle for Mario. When his accountant confirmed that he had made a notable loss in that period, even greater than he expected, he knew his time had come. His accountant suggested that he discuss his options with a business consultant.

The consultant

Mario was skeptical about paying someone $1 350 for their opinion when his friends and family had discussed many options over many months. None of their ideas seemed quite right.

Not wanting to fail, Mario met with the consultant, hoping his recommendations could save his business. The consultant laughed when Mario told him that he only sold apples. This seemed proof positive that the writing was on the wall!

The consultant's report began with plenty of long words and obvious comments about the highly crowded marketplace, lack of product distinction and Mario's lack of buying power due to the size of his small operation. It also suggested that, given the fact that the product was a mere commodity, customer loyalty and repeat business could never be an expectation.

The report somewhat clinically stated that, "all apples are the same; an apple is just an apple." Regardless of who was selling it, price was the only basis on which a business advantage could be gained in the apple market.

All these points where obvious to Mario. However the report also referred to the downturn in the economy. This alone strongly indicated that the entire market for apples would decline as consumers tended to favor less-healthy processed fast foods in times of recession. Unless Mario was prepared to spend money, diversify, reinvent his business and add value to his product, the consultant's recommendation was clear – he would have to close the stall.

Put simply, it was unrealistic to expect to make money from selling one core product. He could not just sell apples. Mario had to offer consumers more and change his business model.

All these elaborate explanations only served to confirm what was already in Mario's mind "the industry is not what it used to be; you can't make money in it anymore; customers only care about price; and there is no loyalty in the world anymore."

Five possible solutions

The consultant's report provided five key suggestions for business reinvention, most of which Mario had already considered.

1. Provide a total solution

Offer a full range of fruits and vegetables giving customers a total "one stop" solution. Invest greater amounts and buy a broader range of products to sell.

Spending more money on products was not a big deal to Mario as he was prepared to do whatever it took to succeed. However, this option presented Mario with a dilemma over his lack of knowledge. Mario knew apples; he was fantastic at picking a good one from a bad one. How then could he suddenly hope to be an expert on all other fruit types? He wouldn't know a good banana when he saw one; much less recognize the difference between a good mango and a poor quality mango.

To make matters worse, how could Mario contemplate selling vegetables as well? They were well outside his knowledge and experience. How could he do the right thing by his customers, expecting them to buy vegetables from him, if he was just an expert apple guy?

2. Become a niche specialist

Develop a niche specialty, dramatically expand the offering and sell other flavors and types of red apples, to carve a niche market. Sell up to seven varieties of red apples with slightly different flavors, or import a few exotic types from the Far East and sell ten varieties.

At first Mario thought this may be something to pursue as he knew apples. The problem with selling ten varieties would mean that he would have to expand his small stall in order to display them all. He was concerned about whether the increase in costs would be offset by more sales. Having to deal with ten different suppliers wouldn't be easy and he wouldn't want to have to rely on ten different people. Continuity of supply was important to him.

Mario's instinct told him that people just wanted to buy a standard apple. Offering ten options would just make things harder for them. He could not see how this approach would help his customers. He stocked and sold the best variety already, so why create confusion for his customers?

The other suggestion was to sell Organic Apples. Mario had already considered this. In fact, he had already tried it in a small way selling some side-by-side with his normal apples, but customers were just not willing to pay three times the price.

3. Source alternate supply

To only sell apples, Mario should change his supplier and import cheaper apples from the Far East. This would enable undercutting of competitors and he would have the cheapest apples in the area.

Mario disapproved of this option as he was loyal to his current supplier who had given exceptionally favorable credit terms when he first started his business. Mario had not forgotten this and therefore didn't consider changing suppliers a viable option.

Furthermore, Mario thought any price advantage would not actually fix the problem. The hyper mart would likely decrease their prices and make a loss on their apples so they could still advertise that they were the cheapest. The others in the market could quickly copy Mario and also import cheaper produce. Within six months he would be in the same position he was currently in.

4. Add value

"Add value" to product by offering freshly crushed apple juice and apple pies. Invest in juicing equipment, a refrigerator and a small oven to bake the pies. Juice and pies would not necessarily be a profit center for several years. The additional capital and running costs to make juice and pies, relative to the money made on drinks and pies, was not significant. Adding value was in offering a total solution in order to sell the core product. Leveraging off the drink and pie sales to sell apples, would maximize net profit.

Mario was happy to invest money, but was bewildered that the solution to his problem was to start other businesses which he knew nothing about. At best these businesses wouldn't even break even for two years and yet somehow would help him sell more apples. Mario's common sense could not see the validity in the "add value" argument.

He did not want to fix his problem by pretending that he was a baker or a drink vendor. He knew that there were many drink stalls and bakers in and near his stall. Mario had no idea about their profitability and perhaps they too were in a similar position to him in dealing with competitors. It was true that neither Mario nor his friends and family had thought of the adding value scenario, but to pay $1 350 for this idea made him feel slightly ill.

5. Expand and consolidate

Buy one or more of the larger competitors (such as Mr. and Mrs. Watson's stall). This approach would achieve economies of scale and see Mario become a bigger player in the market.

Mario didn't feel that buying the stall next door was a sensible option. Mr. and Mrs. Watson's business plan was likely based on upsetting their competitors through low margins to force them to buy them out of the market. Mario knew the Watsons had been selling at price points lower than his, so if he was not making an acceptable profit, they wouldn't be making one either.

To fix an unprofitable business by buying a bigger unprofitable business sounded ridiculous. What was he to do after that, buy the hyper mart? Mario started to get angry about the consultant's lack of common sense.

So, after handing over $1 350 and carefully considering all the consultant's options, Mario had to concede that the end had arrived for his little apple stall. While searching for his business registration documents he discovered a photo his girlfriend had taken of him ten years earlier on the first day he opened the apple stall. A tear came to his eye as he saw the expression of hope and pride on a much younger man's face. Mario felt like a failure and was embarrassed that he hadn't made better use of the startup capital loaned to him by an uncle. Failure didn't feel good, and the reasons for his failure didn't offer Mario any comfort.

A new source of inspiration

That night, after struggling to sleep for hours, Mario awoke with a surprising solution. After thinking about his dilemma for days, inspiration had finally arrived and he frantically began to make notes. Mario had the answer to his business and sales problem!

The photo reminded Mario of many things that had changed over the decade. He was surprised to realize that most of the changes were actually about him. To get things clear in his mind, Mario wrote out an action list for change.

Action list for change

- Replace the cracked and dirty plastic pallet bin displaying the apples with a new wooden oak produce crate.
- Put a red and white checked table cloth between the crate and apples.

6

- Have a bright new stall sign made: "Mario's Apples – 100% fresh."
- Lose the deck chair because there isn't time to sit down.
- Don't read newspapers while waiting for customers.
- Arrive fifteen minutes early and sweep the stall and front walkway.
- Don't look bored behind the stall. Stand, smile and be happy.
- Be proud and confident. Expect people to buy.
- Have a positive attitude.
- Stay at the stall all day, even on slow days.
- Check stock more thoroughly and remove bruised or poor quality apples.
- Use better quality brown paper bags, not cheap white plastic bags.
- Give out samples to entice undecided customers to buy.
- Dress better – blue jeans, white shirt with a clean navy blue apron.
- Review presentation of packaging.
- Install more lighting to brighten the stall.
- Ask people if they want to buy some apples as they pass.
- Thank those who don't and wish them a pleasant day.
- Only close the stall after all customers have left the market.
- Polish and check all apples before going home every night.
- Increase prices.
- Make changes quickly.

Mario got to work on his list and within three days he had all changes in place. He no longer used cheap white plastic bags; instead he used large brown paper bags. He stamped each side with his black print logo which read "Mario's Apples – 100 % Fresh."

As customers watched, Mario deliberately filled each bag with one apple at a time, in a tangible display of care and attention to detail. He then neatly folded down the top of the bag exactly four times before putting a small white sticker to hold it down. Mario had bought the stickers cheaply on the internet and each sticker read "Enjoy – hand checked, supreme quality." Mario took care to have the brown paper bag stand tall without being crumpled; it looked prestigious.

Mario stuck to his plan day after day and did not compromise. Before long, he had to increase his order with his supplier as he was regularly running out of stock. Business picked up to such an extent that people were often waiting to be served.

To counter this, Mario employed an assistant who understood his new standards and why it was so important to follow them. Mario's new assistant brought her own ideas to the stall. She packaged the apples in the paper bag but used a bright red ribbon to tie the bag like a bunch of flowers. The new approach to packaging created interest and increased sales.

Mario then started to use the three days that the market was closed to cold call local businesses and offices. He took bags of apples and asked if people wanted to buy them. Soon the people who bought apples from the offices also attended Mario's stall on market days with their family.

The outcome

Mario's business was not only repaired, but it surpassed all of his expectations in terms of sales, revenue and profit. He was proud of the fact that he did not quit and was not influenced by those around him. Following his changes, he sold more apples in the suburb than any of his competitors and he was confident that he also made the greatest unit margins.

Most of all, Mario was proud about being better at selling his product than the multinational hyper mart. Despite all their advertising and market research using all their vast resources - Mario could outsell them. He sold more apples and at higher prices. Now, as opposed to thinking about closing his stall, he was in the process of opening another one.

Mario didn't change suppliers or products. The market didn't change; it wasn't less competitive. Mario simply realized that the person at the front line could make all the difference to a company's profitability. Through reinventing his own business Mario had come to see that all the promotion and brand awareness in the world is wasted if the front line salesperson doesn't know how to sell – without discounting.

The moral of the story

Whether you sell airplanes, rocket fuel, stocks, shares, insurance, metal cans or apples, it all comes down to the same premise. Do whatever it is that you do, do it well and be the industry expert!

Part 1: Before you start

Knowing what you're doing, where you're going and how you're going to get there will immediately set you apart from most of your sales competitors. Even before you start!

The value of always moving towards your goals with a positive attitude and without wasting your precious time cannot be emphasized enough.

This attitude will help you avoid distractions, frustration and stress on the road to sales success.

In this part:
  What's it all for?
  Positive can do
  It's my job

1.1

What's it all for?

We all need a target, a desired outcome to strive for. And we need to know what the end result of our efforts will deliver. What is it that we want to achieve that will provide a sense of accomplishment and make us feel fulfilled and satisfied? We need to know why we're doing what we're doing so we can maintain motivation.

Everyone's goals are different

At this stage, when talking about our goals and objectives, we're not referring to a desire to be the best sales person in the company, or a desire to do a certain number of sales calls per day. Goals and objectives that relate to your responsibilities as a sales person will be covered later.

Firstly, we're more concerned about larger goals. Who we are, what we want and where we want to go with our life. By clearly understanding who we are and how we want to be, we'll be able to prioritize our time and efforts effectively. Being organized and having clarity about what we're doing and where we're going will help to sustain the impetus needed to maintain motivation when real life throws us off course.

Initially this might seem as if we're making a sales job harder than it needs to be. But by having "big picture" clarity about where you're going will be tremendously helpful in avoiding the "small stuff." Those distracting conversations and other kinds of time-wasting that can throw you off course. It helps you to avoid wasting your time in office politics and worrying about things that shouldn't be your concern or priority.

Taking time to clearly define and document personal goals can help us to identify aspects of our work and personal lives we want to change or improve. This can be a confronting process due to the personal nature of the issues it may evoke. However, it is exactly this type of personal dialogue with ourselves that can help to focus our energies and not let a minute of our precious time slip by.

Work is a large and intricate part of our lives. How we think, operate and conduct ourselves at work is usually similar to the way we are in our private lives. When we lack motivation it can lead us to waste further time and energy. It's therefore crucial to define goals for ourselves both professionally and personally so we can remain focused on achieving success every single day.

Defining your goals

The extent you go to in assessing and documenting personal goals is a personal choice. In the least, think through the points outlined below and you may appreciate our viewpoint on this aspect of sales. This is a basic approach to identifying and setting goals.

Work through the following steps:

1. Think of your current personal circumstances and consider your traits with respect to the following:
   - Past successes & failures
   - Financial assets & liabilities
   - Appearance
   - Health
   - Confidence

2. Consider your general attitude. Are you:
   - Enthusiastic
   - Negative

- Positive
- Focused
- Disciplined
- Content
- Energetic

3. Answer the following:
   - What brings you satisfaction?
   - What brings you a sense of accomplishment?
   - Do you have a sense of purpose?
   - What direction are you currently going in?
   - What direction do you want to go in?

4. Once you've thought about your current situation, you should be able to identify what things cause you dissatisfaction and the qualities you have that you're content with. You should be able to define the things you wish to change and improve about yourself and your current circumstances.

5. Identify a couple of goals or improvements that are important for you to address. In clear terms, write down specific goals in no more than one sentence per goal. We suggest that you don't have more than three initial goals.

6. Under each goal, write a few bullet points that define specific actions, i.e. how you will achieve that goal. It's important to keep your goals and the bullet point actions as brief as possible. There is no benefit in creating complex and intricately detailed goals as they will stand little chance of being achieved.

7. Store your goals in a place you can revisit every week to ensure that you are still on track. When you revisit your list of goals, ask yourself:

- Did I stay focused on my goal and actions?
- What are the reasons that I achieved or didn't achieve my goals?

Goal / Objective	Actions Required
Donate 10% of Gross Income to Charity to Help Less Fortunate Strangers	• Create personal budget • Identfy a charity to support • Open a new bank account for automatic money transfers
Run a half Marathon in a foreign country	• Identify a city with a marathon to attend • Surpass year-to-date sale budget so as to afford training time • Leave work early Tuesdays & Thursdays to train
Own and Drive a Luxury German-made vehicle	• Establish cost and type of vehicle desired • Investigate finance options and tax implications • Save required deposit • Buy vehicle

Having successfully completed this exercise the first time you'll be able to build on what you've learnt the next. In future goal setting sessions you'll be able to use the same process to further define your goals, set more goals and assess your progress at appropriate intervals.

You may find it useful to take a step back every twelve months and consider the wider issues and themes outlined in steps one, two and three.

What's this got to do with sales?

Understandably this self assessment may initially appear to be the domain of a life coach or personal motivator, with little real world application to the life of a sales person.

By taking time to consider yourself and identify what is truly important to you, the attainment of these important goals will bring you genuine satisfaction and a feeling of success – as opposed to the short-term gratification of being in first place on this month's sales tally board.

If you have an awareness of what you're setting out to achieve then you'll be more positive, proactive, disciplined and motivated in your daily actions and in the use of time. This closely relates to your sales work. By appreciating your sales role as being part of a vehicle which will deliver you to achieving other, more important and critical personal goals you'll be less distracted in your sales work.

If you understand, for example, that you want to be the best sales person in your company because it will provide maximum financial return and in turn assist you to achieve the lifestyle goals that are important to you, then you'll be more self-motivated, focused and enthusiastic.

A sales person's role requires a proactive approach to their tasks and their use of time. You are the driver, not the passenger.

For example, a customer service support person or a book keeper's role is reactive in nature as they must respond to the existing problems that await them. Their day involves following and taking directions and is largely driven by events and the actions of others.

In stark contrast, a sales person's role doesn't involve clearly-defined tasks for completion. By its very nature, it's a role that must be proactive in creating daily work plans and tasks. The lack of specific direction and instruction can be difficult for some sales people to come to terms with.

Fundamentally, a sales person has three choices when they leave the office. They can:

- Call on existing or potential customers;
- Go see a movie; or
- Drink coffee at a shopping mall.

In the end, you need to decide if you're a driver of your own actions with the ability to maintain your own motivation. Having clear goals helps you to be motivated.

All good things take time

A sales person often receives the gratification of obtaining a sales order long after they have done the hard work, the sustained sales activity. In some sales scenarios a customer sales order may only be obtained after many months, or even years of diligent sales work. The delayed gratification inherent in a sales role makes the ability to sustain and self-motivate critical to your success while you wait to enjoy the benefits of your hard work.

Be careful about what motivates you

Don't be motivated by the desire to gain acceptance from those around you. Most people seem to settle for average or aspire to be slightly better than average. Be individual in the standards that you set for yourself. There is nothing extraordinary about being common. Yes it can be lonely at the top, but the view may be fantastic with plenty of options and choices. Why would you want to miss it?

I.2

Positive can do

Few things are as powerful as the actions that result from a view of the world driven by naive optimism.

To be successful in a sales role your view of the world and your attitude must be set to positive!

Success will be determined by your ability to have and maintain a positive "can do" attitude towards achieving your goals and sales objectives.

The way you choose to look at the world makes all the difference between success and failure. A drinking glass is half filled with water. In sales, the glass is always half full. It is never, ever seen to be half empty. Always choose a positive viewpoint.

It is wrong to rationalize your thought process as being "realistic"; you must genuinely believe the glass to be half full without qualification.

Your positive can do attitude

To be successful in sales you need to be *enthusiastic* about your job. Sales is not a job that you can just *do*. You have to *want* to do it. Not only must you want to do it, you need to be enthusiastic about doing it or it won't work for you. Having a positive mindset will help facilitate your enthusiasm.

Dedication is also a vital attribute you'll need to be successful in a sales role. Your commitment to push through barriers is mandatory for sales success. Again, these characteristics are more readily employed from a positive rather than a negative view of the world.

You need a *good work ethic* to find sales success. Sales success does not find you. You have to work in order to find it. Your positive can do attitude helps deliver an eagerness to do what needs to be done; a good work ethic is harder to generate without a positive impetus.

You need to be *passionate* about your role and how you set about performing what is required of you. Being positive and "can do" about things helps to facilitate passion. Without a positive attitude, passion is hard to unveil.

Be passionate, never emotional

You're paid to do a job, so do that job and leave your emotions at home. Be enthusiastic and passionate, but leave emotional responses aside. Being emotional will distract you and limit your sales success. Your positive can do attitude guides you in understanding the difference between being productively passionate and emotionally time-wasting.

Always be passionate, never be emotional.

It's not optional

You must think positively.

You must be enthusiastic.

You must be dedicated.

You must believe that you can succeed.

You must be passionate.

To be successful in sales, these traits aren't optional. They can't be compromised.

Opportunity, an appropriate by-product

Consider the available opportunity for you to sell your product and succeed in your sales role:

- Can you see a scale of opportunity which is too great to take advantage of?
- Can you see more potential customers than available time to approach them all?
- Do you feel frustrated or overwhelmed by the volume of options available to pursue?
- Are you unsure where to start, given the number of potential customers you could do business with?

Having a positive attitude and a positive frame of mind will lead you to seeing a vast scale of opportunity that is too enormous for you to individually take advantage of. In fact, armed with a positive can do attitude you'll be able to see that there is always too much opportunity available to all of us.

Business is a game
In addition to a positive can do attitude, you should also consider business to be a game. It's a sport that you are playing. We're not involved in life and death decisions, we're not confronted with sickness and sadness as we conduct our daily tasks. Considering the misfortune some people experience in the world, there is no such thing as "having a bad day" when you're working in sales.

Enjoy what you do and have fun in your work. This view of your role will ensure you take the right perspective to help form your attitude. You should still want to win, you should still want to beat all your competitors, but it's a game that we play, so enjoy it.

You should never give up or compromise, but it's not life or death.

Accountability, the perfect companion to positivity
Your positive can do attitude should also have a strong element of accountability. You need to hold yourself accountable and see this as your responsibility, not someone else's.

This attitude will help you surpass competitors and colleagues. You have two responsibilities. One is to your employer and those employees not directly involved in sales functions. You're responsible for selling the products and services so that your organization will be profitable and prosper. Your colleagues may work very hard to provide you with products and the support required, so you shouldn't disappoint or be disrespectful of their efforts. You're accountable to your company and work colleagues to perform successfully in your sales role.

Your second responsibility is for your own actions and use of your time. When confronted with any issue or frustration you must look firstly in the mirror and ask what you can do or change to improve the situation. Never look to apportion blame to others. Always take responsibility for your own actions.

As part of this accountability to yourself you are also responsible for your own improvement and your education. Don't wait for others to teach or help you; you need to proactively be accountable to yourself for improving your sales ability.

A sales person's role is very different to most other roles in any organization. When a worker or manager in a company makes a mistake it is usually discovered through the conduct of business or through the company's systems or procedures. When a sales person makes a mistake in the customer's office by saying the wrong thing and losing a sale because of this, no one else in the sales person's company ever see the error.

For this reason you have to self-assess your performance and identify things you could or should have done better or differently on each sales call.

Display your positivity

Your positive attitude must be highly visible to your customer. Few, if any sales people have found success by depressing or boring a customer into buying from them!

Assume for a moment that all products in your industry are essentially the same and that there is very little, if any, difference between your product and your competitors' offering. What reason would any customer have to choose your solution over the next sales person's solution?

That reason is *you*. You would be the only difference between the options the potential customer has. Your approach, style, delivery and even your choice of words has a significant impact on the customer's decision. So if you appreciate how much impact you have in every sales opportunity, you will quickly understand the need to display a positive outlook.

You're on your own
Only you can deliver your positive attitude. Your manager, colleagues or associates are all unable to assist you. You have to deliver it on your own. Others around you can show you what it looks like, but no one can help you deliver a positive can do attitude.

Be an elite athlete
If you select a role model or someone to aspire to do not pick the guy or gal in the next cubical who is better than you at some things. Be the elite athlete in your field. Learn from the elite business person or sports team that you admire. Take lessons from the highly-accomplished and use their actions to remind you how to have a positive can do attitude in all that you do.

It's a mindset
Having a positive can do attitude is not a fancy suit, a forced fast walk, an inspirational poster or about using power words. It's a mindset, a view of the world, a perspective that should be evident in your achievements.

A positive attitude is what opens your eyes; it is the heartbeat to your success. Eventually it will subconsciously precede every thought and action.

Possessing a positive can do attitude will deliver you most of the way to success.

A positive attitude will help you see business as a sport, where opportunities overwhelmingly outweigh your available time. It helps you to hold yourself accountable for your responsibilities, without the need for other peoples' input.

Believe in yourself and in your abilities and look to maximize every opportunity. You will be astounded by the results.

1.3

It's my job

While this may seem too obvious to discuss, it's essential that you clearly understand your role.

You're employed to generate income for the business that you're representing.

Your role is not about generating revenue, turnover or gross sales value.

Sales people are employed to generate profit for the business. While turnover and unit sales are often used as key measures of performance, fundamentally they're always a secondary priority. That's because these things don't pay the bills.

It's all about profit

The profit that you generate must be greater than the personal remuneration paid to you by the business owner(s).

Not only must your actions generate sufficient revenue to pay for your remuneration, but your efforts must also contribute to the overall costs and profitability of the business.

This and this alone is the reason that you are employed.

No other person in your organization is there to generate profit in such a direct and deliberate manner. Others are there to take care of administration, coordinate resources and to control business costs. But their work is generated after action is taken by the sales department. Without sales they wouldn't have any reason to be there.

As a sales person, your ability to "sell" is a key factor in determining your company's ultimate profitability. If you can sell more units, can hold sales margin in both the selling price of your product, as well as hold appropriate margin in any after sale service pricing, this will quickly and directly impact your company's profitability.

You should be appropriately remunerated and you must personally benefit from the value you add to the company, but you should understand that your obligation is to obtain company profit, not merely cover your personal remuneration.

"Sales person" can mean many things

"Sales person" is a common label, encompassing many different role types. Let's look at some of the possibilities.

Retail sales person

The sales person or shop assistant waits for customers to come into their shop or showroom. Typically these are domestic consumers, not people buying for business needs.

Reactive sales person

The majority of customers come to the sales person and this in turn may lead to some follow-up sales effort by that person, for example, a car sales person or someone selling houses. These types of sales people mostly sell to domestic consumers, with only some sales to business customers.

Business-to-business sales person

The sales person is typically engaged in selling low-value commodity items where large quantities of a product are typically sold to a given customer. They proactively call on their customers, but they could be categorized as merchandisers, rather than sales people.

The sales person has limited power to affect the outcome and limited ability to personally increase the number of customers buying from their company as a result of their personal effort. Their personal effort may however influence the volume that a given customer purchases, for example, food and beverage manufacturers selling to large retail outlets.

Business-to-business direct sales person

Involves the movement of higher-value products where the number of products sold to a given customer is typically low. Sales people proactively visit customers (current and potential). The number of potential customers is always greater than the number of current customers.

The sales person has the freedom to approach potential customers, as opposed to waiting for the customer to come to them. Once potential customers are identified they can be secured through the efforts of the sales person. The sales person's individual efforts can have a notable impact on the company's profitability.

This type of sales person is typical for most business-to-business sales.

The business-to-business direct sales person has the greatest scope to seek new business, negotiate with customers and grow their employer's business.

In this book, we will address a business-to-business direct sales person's role as this is the most complicated; other sales roles can take lessons as appropriate for their role.

Regardless of the type of sales person you are, you're not employed for any other reason than to profitably sell as many products as possible in your market. You do this by proactively approaching current and potential customers.

Are you "marketing" or "selling"?

Appreciating the difference between "marketing" and 'selling" is often confusing for people new to a sales role. In very simple terms, a marketing department has the function of creating brand awareness. They promote the brand and attempt to entice potential customers. The sales department's function is to convert any interest into a commercial transaction, i.e. to obtain an order from the potential customer, thereby turning them into a customer. The sales department is responsible for affecting the transaction.

All the brand awareness in the world is of no value if the potential customer does not place an order. To understand the importance of a sales person within a commercial company, ask yourself if a company can survive without a sales department or without a marketing department. Which department can survive without the other?

If a sales person has both the drive and communication skills they can seek and secure sales orders without the need for a marketing department. They don't need to rely on a prospect's brand awareness in order to create sales leads.

A sales person approaches potential customers to create interest in and awareness of their product. The extent to which this holds true is a function of the value and nature of the product. But the point is this. Many companies prosper by employing sales people to go to their potential customers; they don't wait for an enquiry to be created by a marketing department. This tends to be a more cost-effective method of obtaining business-to-business sales.

In fact, many sales people who don't have marketing departments may benefit from the marketing done by their competitors. A sales person can obtain the customer's sales order by being better at their craft than the sales person working for the company that conducted the marketing.

Customers comparing options will look at alternatives that are available in the market. So, the organized sales person, who goes to a potential customer, may find themselves up against competitors that have engaged in marketing. If the sales person can tell a better story and outline how their option is a better choice, they can secure the customer's order. This is despite the fact that the customer was brought into the market by competitor marketing and advertising.

Generally speaking, a marketing department is not mandatory, but a sales department is, especially where business-to-business selling is concerned.

Treat it like your business

Implied in your role is a requirement to always act as if it was your business, i.e. as if you owned the business that employs you. Act as if it was your money at stake.

If it *was* your business, would you be adamant about taking your extended lunch break? Would you make that extra sales call before stopping for the day? Would you innovate, suggest improvements and provide feedback from the customers?

If you think like a business owner this will lead you to the most opportunity and rewards a sales role can provide.

A profitable profession

Being a good sales person can be one of the most secure and profitable professions available. There is always demand for people who can create business, regardless of economic conditions. A professional sales person will work autonomously and will view their sales territory (the geographic or market segment that they are responsible for) as their own business.

In effect, they should view it as a business within a business.

Demand for good sales people who can create new business by generating sales never subsides.

Oh, and don't forget...

Finally, it's critical to understand that you're only "as good as your last game."

Your past performance will not pay this month's bills and company expenses. In sales you are only as good as last month's sales performance.

More directly than any other role in your organization, a sales person is responsible and accountable for profit.

You're employed to sell at profitable price points and are account-able for ensuring business costs can be paid from the sales you transact. It's not about sales turnover; it's all about profitable sales. And selling profitably each and every month!

Quick recap: Before you start

Your goals
It can be difficult to maintain motivation every single day in the face of lost orders, family issues or business pressures. Understand what's im-portant to you and what you want to achieve in your life.

By identifying clear goals it's easier to be motivated to accomplish those daily small tasks and actions that will carry you towards achieving what's truly important to you.

Your approach
A sales person's role requires a proactive approach to their tasks and their use of time. You are the driver, not the passenger.

You must think positively.

You must be enthusiastic.

You must be dedicated.

You must believe that you can succeed.

You must be passionate.

To be successful in sales, these traits aren't optional. They can't be compromised.

Your attitude
Possessing a positive can do attitude will deliver you most of the way to success.

A positive attitude will help you see business as a sport, where op-portunities overwhelmingly outweigh your available time. It helps you to hold yourself accountable for your responsibilities, without the need for other people's input.

Believe in yourself and in your abilities and look to maximize every opportunity. You'll be astounded by the results.

Your job

The profit that you generate must be greater than the personal remuneration paid to you by the business owner(s).

Not only must your actions generate sufficient revenue to pay for your remuneration, but your efforts must also contribute to the overall costs and profitability of the business.

This and this alone is the reason that you are employed.

Part 2: The 7 steps of a sale

Every sale, particularly in a business-to-business context, has a natural series of steps. By understanding these phases of a given sale, you can act accordingly to position your product or solution in the customer's mind as the most preferred option to select.

By appreciating the sale as a series of steps, you not only maximize the chance of securing the order from the customer, but it helps you sell at higher price points, obtaining higher gross profit.

In this part:
Stepping through a sale
The numbers game
You can't store sleep
The first date
Entertain me
The proposal
Let's talk
Signed, sealed and ordered
Sorry about your loss

2.1

Stepping through a sale

Every sale goes through a series of steps or a structured process. Appreciating the steps of the sale and acting accordingly will translate into increased sales and sales with better financial return.

The essence of the sales process (the steps of a sale) can be characterized as follows:

Step 1:   Who can we help?

Step 2:   How can we help you?
            What do we need to fix or improve for you?
            How can we make things better for you?

Step 3:   This is how we can help you.
            This is our product and solution.

Step 4:   In summary, this is what you want or need to change and improve, here's how we can help and this is what you'll need to pay.

Step 5:   Not quite sure yet?
            You seem to have concerns, what are they?
            Let me understand, explain and clarify.

Step 6:   An order is placed. Thank you for buying from us.

Step 7:   No order. You have purchased from someone else!
            May we ask why?

Whatever title you prefer to use for each step is academic, so long as you appreciate that there are distinct stages for a sale – from locating a customer to securing a sales order.

Step 1 – Lead generation

The first step is about finding someone to sell to, someone who is, or should be in the market for your product or solution. We mainly concern ourselves with what action you can take as a sales person to generate a sales lead. This is called cold-calling, prospecting, farming, canvassing and many other names.

Lead generation performed by a sales person can take the following forms:

- Cold-calling – physically attending, without invitation, a potential customer's premises.
- Telemarketing – telephoning a potential customer.
- Mailers – letter drops, posted letters, flyers, hard copy and 3D mailers, etc.
- Calling upon current customers with a view to upgrading or selling them additional products or solutions.
- Social media or electronic marketing activity conducted by the sales person.

Obviously there are many forms of marketing and promotion that can be conducted by the company which may not be created by a sales person's direct efforts.

Step 2 – First appointment

A first appointment is the first chance we get to meet a potential customer and to establish what it is they need or want, if anything. This could be called a "needs analysis" meeting.

While this discussion can take place over the telephone or via email, it is best that this is a face-to-face meeting. Meeting with your customer in person is the best way to communicate with them as it enables you to understand what their situation is by seeing it for yourself. You also get a chance to appreciate their body language and will better understand the situation – as opposed to only hearing what they're saying. We'll elaborate on this as we work through the steps of the sale.

Step 3 – Demonstration

We call this step a demonstration because we use this stage to display our product to the customer.

We show them why they should select our option as opposed to selecting a competitor's offering, or the option of retaining their current solution. Where possible, we invite the customer to touch, feel, see or experience the product so they better understand what we're offering. It should be more than a mere explanation, value proposition or sales pitch. It's not just "talk", it's "show and tell."

Step 4 – The proposal

A proposal is the step where we summarize the issues our customer wants addressed, outline how our product and solution will address the issues they've raised and will improve their situation. We also explain what the investment cost will be, i.e. how much they have to pay.

Step 5 – Negotiation

This is when the customer has questions or you address any concerns they may have with proceeding with your proposed solution. Discussions could be about the product, the after sale service and support, or the payment method you're requiring the customer to commit to.

Step 6 – Order
The potential customer places an order and agrees to purchase from you, thereby becoming your *actual* customer.

Step 7 – Lost order
This is the most forgotten step of the sales process. When you don't receive the order from a customer because they selected an alternate supplier it's not a pleasant feeling. This step of establishing and understanding why the customer selected another option is often ignored by sales people, but is exceptionally valuable in determining their long term success.

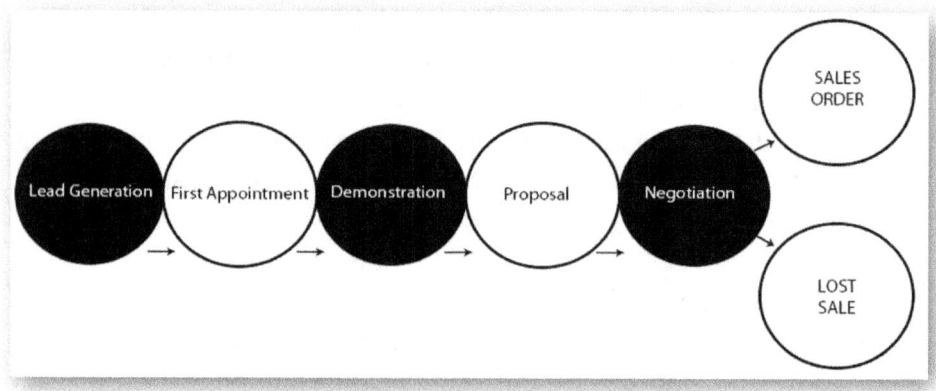

What are the steps of the sale for your product?
Consider the clichéd sales person – selling vacuum cleaners door-to-door. In this example the steps of the sale are self evident:

1. Door knocking, house-to-house, door-to-door.
2. Has discussion with the potential customer asking them what they currently use to vacuum.

3. Demonstrates product ability and the differences between the customer's current mode of operation and their product and solution (a proof statement).
4. Provides price and payment plan options.
5. Addresses any concerns or objections the customer may have to buying.
6. Obtains an order to purchase.

It need not be a physically tangible product, but the same process will usually apply to the product or solution that you sell.

Consider a finance broker who sells business finance.

1. Approaches businesses seeking appointments and offering services.
2. Obtains an appointment to discuss business finance requirements and identifies current and potential customer needs.
3. Outlines a solution and shows an example of how their finance facility operates. Also has detailed discussion on how interest is calculated and early termination exit fees are enacted. Provides copies of finance contracts with highlighted fine print of typical industry contracts, as well as their own finance contract. Finally, provides written references from existing customers.
4. Clearly documents their finance facility agreement.
5. Discusses customer-specific concerns and objections.
6. Obtains initial order from customer.

Take a moment to identify the steps of a typical sale of a product or solution within your industry. You'll find you can also break down your sale process into these steps.

How long do the steps take?

Usually, the higher the value of expenditure required, the longer it takes to complete the steps. However, generally speaking, there is no typical length of time, as the customer's particular circumstance is the most significant factor. The more pressing the customer's need, the greater the sense of urgency they have to make a buying decision. It could take one hour or more than one year, there's no set rule or expectation.

Keeping track

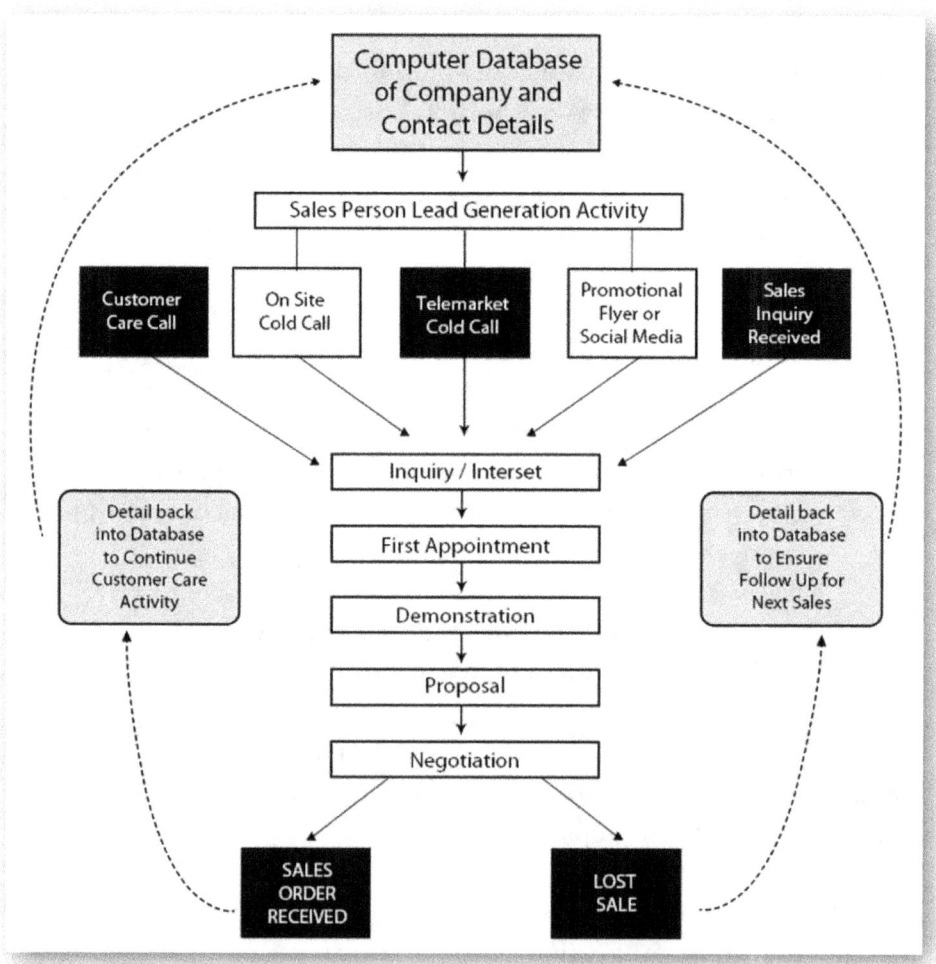

Following and managing all your customers and potential customers requires significant organization and time management skills.

As they're all at different stages of the selling cycle, it's your ability to multi-task that holds the key to capitalizing on all your hard work by not neglecting any of the sale opportunities.

There are many computer software programs that can help you organize and track all your sales activity. Having to remember all the contacts you need to follow up – who are at different stages of the selling cycle – can be overwhelming.

Databases are valuable in coordinating your efforts and ensuring that nothing is overlooked in terms of your follow-up. They can assist sales people who aren't naturally organized to be in control of their entire sales territory and minimize the risk of missing out on a potential sales order.

Try to keep your database as simple as possible with a minimum amount of detail. You should view the database as a tool to remind you who to contact and when to contact them in order to follow up all potential customers. Remember, your database is a means to a financial end; it's not an end in itself. Never forget you're paid on sales, not your ability to collect and record information.

Some employers require database input of customers and potential business to manage product supply and this is valid to assist with stock control and supply of services. Always be mindful that the database is there to help you be *where* it counts, *when* it counts. It's not there to justify your actions or use of time. Your steady flow of sales orders will justify that!

Are the steps distinct from one another?

The key is to see them as separate steps within each sale. They may not be separate encounters or separate meetings, but the sale tends to follow the same process if done right. You need to be mindful of the sentiment of following the steps of the sale.

To appear credible, you can't propose a solution before you understand the customer's needs and issues. You can't sell the attributes of your solution until you understand what aspect of your offer is important to the customer. All steps may occur within one meeting, or it may take several meetings before you can work your way through the sale and secure a profitable order.

That makes sense, but *my* product is easy to sell

Your product might be easy to sell, but regardless of its complexity, we believe that adhering to the sentiment of following the seven steps, it will improve the quantity and profitability of your sales. That's because you'll be setting yourself apart from your competitors.

We follow the steps for two main reasons.

Firstly, you need to know which solution you are going to sell to the customer. By taking the time to ask about the customer's circumstances you can then understand what they need to buy. You're also able to sell the benefits of your solution that are important to them.

You rarely have the time to launch into a generic sales presentation that outlines every feature, advantage and benefit your solution provides, so it makes sense to follow the steps so you know what solution and what parts of that solution are most important to your customer. By speaking to your customer about issues that affect them it will set you apart from your competitors who are largely selling generic sales advantages.

Furthermore, as you've impressed the customer and are ahead of your competitors their preference for your offering will lead to them being more willing to accept the higher price points you may be requesting.

The second main reason for following the steps of the sale is for you to gain an appreciation of how the customer thinks and how they feel about the products they are considering. You're able to ascertain the best way to communicate with them in terms they understand and appreciate.

In addition to understanding *what* you are going to sell you will also understand *how* you should sell your product to the particular customer. Knowing how to sell to a given customer will lead to a situation where you'll have a higher success rate of sales, as well as being able to demand a higher price point than your competitor.

The people sport

Sales is a "people sport." In many industries, people make a decision to buy based on their feeling about a sales person before they consider which company or product they desire. As we're selling to differentiate ourselves from our competitors, in order for the customer to favor our solution, we set ourselves apart by marginally changing how we present to each customer we encounter.

By following the steps of the sale we'll learn what's important to the customer, what their business is all about and how they think or what they value when making decisions. Knowing these intangibles and communicating in a manner that is comfortable to them helps us present in a way that has greater appeal to them.

The product may be identical from all suppliers, but if we tailor how we present (in addition to what we present) to each customer, in line with what they consider important, we are maximizing our chance of obtaining a profitable sales order.

Tell me again, I'm still not convinced

Each day, you'll deal with an infinite variety of customer types. By personalizing the sale your success rate will be at its highest and you'll be seen as a superior option to those you're competing against. If the customer considers you to have a superior offering then you will have the greatest chance of obtaining the sales order, as well as being able to command a higher payment.

Consider two sales people selling business insurance. Assume for a moment that each one has only one product type they can supply and these products are identical.

Sales person one has a first appointment with the customer and they deliver an excellent sales presentation, one that outlines all the features, advantages and benefits of their product. They also display a thorough knowledge of their industry, their product and its applications.

Sales person one is so customer-focused that at the end of the hour-long first appointment they take out their price book and advise the customer what the cost of the policy will be. During their meeting sales person one correctly conveys an implied message that they're too busy to return for a subsequent appointment due to the demand for their solution.

In isolation, they impressed the customer and had an excellent appointment. The meeting ends with the customer thinking that following approval to purchase from their supervisor they will buy the policy from sales person one.

Sales person two uses the hour-long first appointment to ask multiple, in-depth questions about the customer's business and requirements. In fact, all the questions prompted the customer to consider scenarios and situations they had not yet envisaged.

Sales person two ended the meeting by advising the customer that they'll consider the best option for them and return with a recommendation. At the following meeting, sales person two had a further opportunity to build rapport with their potential customer. Their presented solution was priced considerably higher than that proposed by sales person one, but the recommendation was accompanied by several customer-specific benefits. This made the price differential understandable and consequently irrelevant. Sales person two also presented examples of how the policy helped others in a similar situation involving unforeseen circumstances.

Which one would you pick?

Which solution would a customer most likely select? One that was presented exceptionally well, but contained mostly generic sales advantages, or a solution containing advantages that accommodated the customer's needs more precisely?

Is an option presented by a sales person who appeared to be a diligent industry professional favored over a flawless presentation from a very good sales person? Which type of person would the customer feel more comfortable dealing with? Which person would the customer feel safer buying from?

In both scenarios, the product was the same, but the way in which it was sold can make all the difference to who wins the sales order. Sales person two was seen as more thorough and diligent, so it may appear to be a safer bet to go with this sales person. The emotions that sales person one generated in the customer subsided over the selling cycle. The patient sales person two would win the sales order, despite having a higher selling price.

Sales person two had a greater chance to sell to the customer by having two visits and yes, it did take more time. But by obtaining a new customer, sales person two can more easily sell products to this customer in the future, an opportunity that doesn't exist if the first sale is not secured.

2.2

The numbers game

While the selling cycle is a series of distinct stages, the old adage of "sales is a numbers game" still holds true.

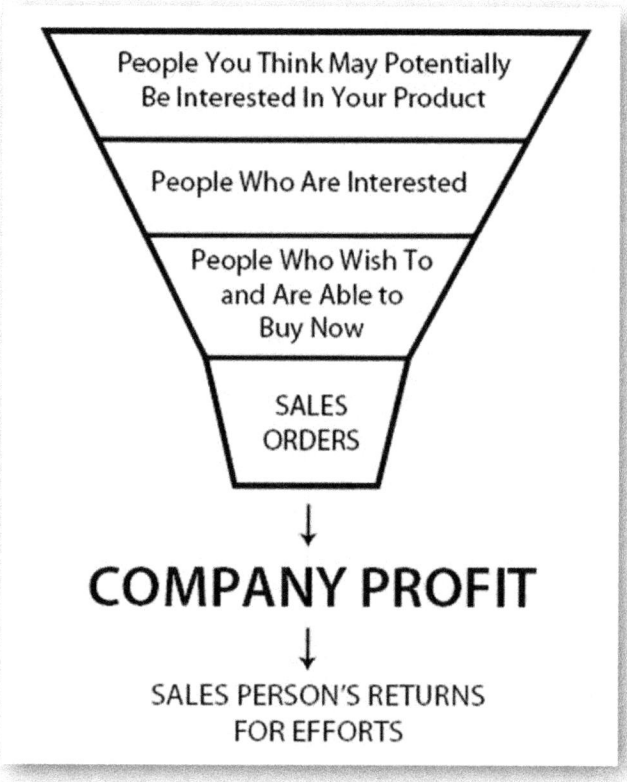

People You Think May Potentially Be Interested In Your Product

People Who Are Interested

People Who Wish To and Are Able to Buy Now

SALES ORDERS

↓

COMPANY PROFIT

↓

SALES PERSON'S RETURNS FOR EFFORTS

The greater number of leads you generate through lead generation, the greater the number of appointments you'll be able to make with potential customers. From these first appointments some potential customers will be keen for you to demonstrate your product or solution. This, in turn, will lead to you providing them with a proposal. Logically, the greater the number of proposals you present, the more negotiations you will have, leading to the likelihood of you obtaining more orders.

Here's another way to view the steps of the sale:

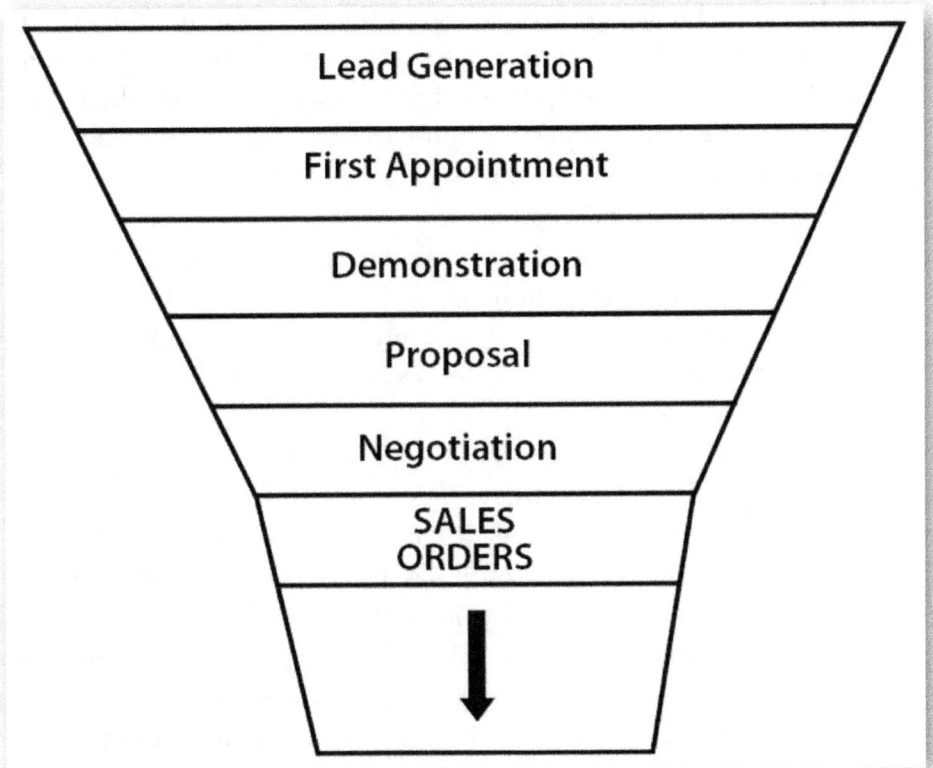

The power of numbers

Even a very small amount of lead generation activity conducted by a sales person, typically called "prospecting", can quickly become effective.

Consider this scenario which includes the following conservative assumptions:

- A sales person makes two appointments in the morning and two appointments in the afternoon, four days per week.
- For each appointment the sales person attends they also conduct three cold calls (refer to the "You can't store sleep" chapter). They cold call businesses close to their appointment since they are already there and have a few moments to spare. Alternately, the sales person telephones three companies (from their data-base) when they return to their car; this is also a financially and logistically feasible option.
- Conservatively, let's assume:
  - Only 1 in every 60 potential customers contacted is in the market right now.
  - Only 4 in every 60 potential customers contacted is in the market within the next 6-18 months.
  - It then follows:
    - In one day = 4 appointments x 3 cold calls = 12 cold calls.
    - In one week = 4 days x 12 cold calls = 48 cold calls.
    - In one month = 4.33 weeks in a month x 48 cold calls = 207 cold calls.
- So, in a given month the sales person can effortlessly conduct 207 cold calls in addition to all their other work.
- After say, a 12-month period, in every month, as a result of conducting three cold calls around each appointment the following would apply:

- 3.45 potential customers are in the market <u>now</u>
  (207 calls in a month with 1 in 60 in the market <u>now</u>
  = 207÷60 = 3.45 potential customers per month in the
  market <u>now</u>).
- 13.8 potential customers are now in the market formally
  <u>within 6-18 months</u>
  (207 calls in a month with 4 in 60 in the market <u>within</u>
  <u>6-18 months</u> = 207÷60 = 3.45; 3.45 x 4 = 13.8 potential
  customers in the market <u>within 6-18 months</u>.)
- 17 new potential customers are in the market at the start
  of each and every month
  (3.45 in the market <u>now</u> + 13.8 in the market <u>within 6-18</u>
  <u>months</u> = 17.25).

If you were to deal with 17 new potential customers at the start of
each month then each year you would be proposing your solution to 204
potential customers. That's almost one new customer per business day.
Keep in mind that this is in addition to your other work.

Regardless of your ability and conversion rates (how many sales
you achieve compared to the number of potential customers you deal
with), dealing with this many potential new customers each and every month (some of whom may require more than one product) may
mean you need a full-time assistant to give you a chance of keeping
up!

We're not including current customer sales enquiries, or sales enquiries received from other sources. We're only including the lead generation the sales person happened to generate themselves as they did a few
cold calls while completing their other tasks.

It is worth noting again that the numbers and ratios used in this
example are *very* conservative. However, it still suggests that even with a
consistent and small volume of cold calling, a notable volume of potential sales can be generated.

Naturally the above applies to product types that can be sold to most businesses. Industry-specific scenarios should be acknowledged here. The number of cold calls for a sales person selling say, wind turbines or cat scan equipment, may be closer to three or four, as opposed to twelve a week. But in the context of their industry they will have the same effect by increasing the enquiry rate – as opposed to waiting for enquiries to be received.

How much is sold in your industry?

Take a moment to think about how many competitors are selling in your sales territory (here we refer to your sales territory, not your company's total sales area).

How many units do you think each competitor would sell in your sales territory in a given month? If you multiply your most conservative estimate by the number of competing companies you will quickly appreciate the total volume of business available within your sales territory.

If at the start of every month you have 17 new potential customers in the market, plus any sales leads that you may have been provided with, plus any referrals, plus any customer sales enquiries, it's not hard to see that you'll soon be overwhelmed!

It might be tempting to think that doing 12 prospecting cold calls a day is either not physically possible, or unnecessary due to all your other daily activities. However, it is more profitable to consider a positive not a negative solution. Perhaps employ a sales assistant to do all your administration and follow up tasks? In turn, this will lead to more efficiencies and the ability to create even more business and earn even more income.

The more success you create, the more success finds you as potential customers will start to seek you out when you're the dominant player in your field.

Let's take one further step

There's no avoiding the fact that sales is a "numbers game." The more potential customers we have, the more potential sales we can make.

Every supplier tends to have a natural market segment where they're able to gain more success. These are market segments where they have the best competitive advantage.

Your lead generation activity should be focused on those potential customers where you can receive the best financial return for your effort. Always specifically target the more profitable potential customers within your natural market segment.

Think of things in these terms: A good fisherman does not earn their reputation through all types of fishing. He may be good at one of the following, but not all:

- Fishing off the end of the pier.
- Beach fishing.
- Deep sea line fishing.
- Net fishing

The same applies in business. You may have a product that can be sold to all market segments, but limit your proactive effort to pursuing those market segments that are the most profitable, i.e. potential customers who understand and appreciate your competitive advantage story.

If you pursue all potential customers you are changing your sales funnel in the following manner:

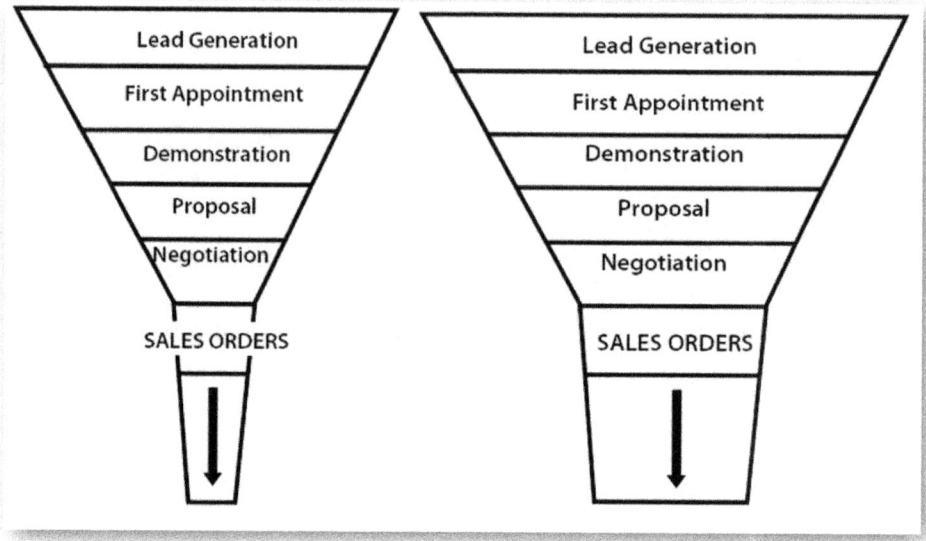

Naturally, increased lead generation activity will result in greater sales success.

If you reduce your volume of lead generation by, say, 20% and only actively pursue your more profitable market segment, you can devote that extra 20% of energy to building and improving your sales skills. This approach will provide greater success as your superior sales skills will mean you lose fewer deals (sales orders).

Your sales funnel will change as follows:

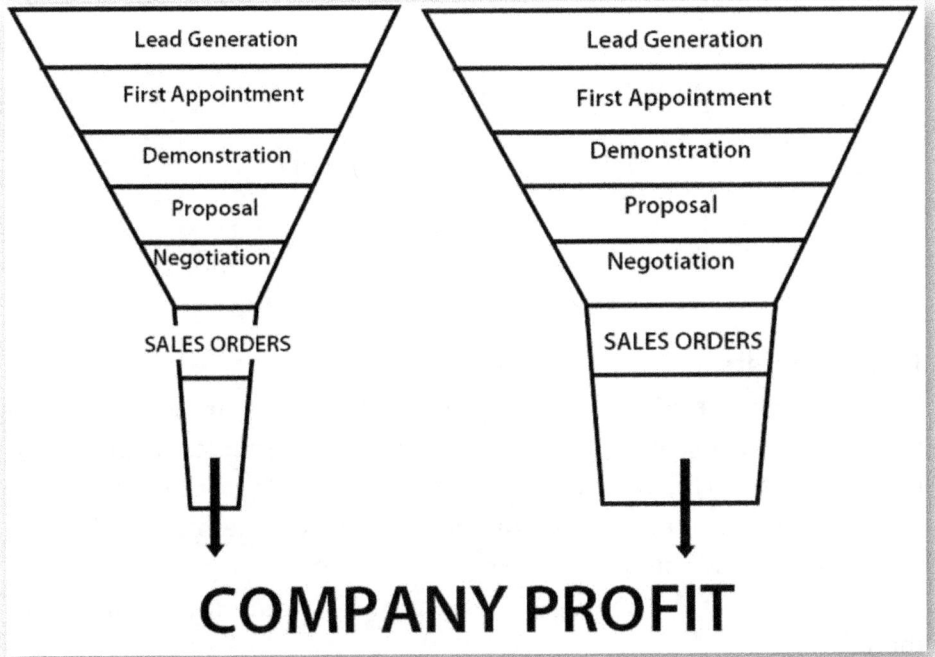

For example, you may not actively pursue an industry type that is typically price-sensitive. You should still follow up all enquiries you receive from that industry, but use your time wisely by not actively pursuing lower profit in more difficult market segments.

The more things change, the more they stay the same

As technology changes and new theories about creating demand for your product come and go, it's easy to be misled into thinking that there's a better way to find and persuade customers. While at times new technology may provide more options for sales people to communicate, the "sales is a numbers game" principle still holds true.

2.3

You can't store sleep

Lead generation

"You can't store sleep" is probably the best way to remind the professional sales person how they need to view lead generation activity. It must be done in small amounts each and every day; otherwise things will not work optimally. If we don't have any lead generation activity we won't have any potential customers.

This stage of the selling cycle cannot be avoided, nor underestimated.

A sales lead or sales enquiry can come in one of two ways:

- A potential customer contacts you.
- You contact a potential customer.

When a potential customer contacts you, the enquiry can be:

- From a referral; someone referred to your company as a result of another customer's experience.
- As a result of marketing activity, such as online advertising, phone directory listings, direct mail promotions, magazine advertisements, radio sponsorship, etc.
- From a current customer who requires additional products because their current product needs updating or renewing.

Alternately, they may have an additional requirement for a product you supply.

To a large extent, you have very little direct control over the number of enquiries you receive. You might receive a referral or an enquiry as a result of previous sales, but this is highly unpredictable. A sales person cannot plan for, or expect to receive a certain number of enquiries on a given day.

As we know, in successful business we mainly want to concern ourselves with what we can do and plan to do to obtain a desired result. Waiting for the phone to ring is never part of a successful business plan!

You should view an enquiry as luck and consider it an unexpected bonus. As you have no direct influence on the enquiry rate you can't take credit for it as if it was a result of your hard work. Fortunately, any enquiry received is a new potential customer that you didn't have to work for, but you now have a chance to convert into a sale.

You contact the potential customer in order to:

- Upgrade a current customer to a newer version of your product.
- Sell additional products to a current customer.
- Obtain new business (a potential customer not currently dealing with your organization).

Why is it up to me?

Generally speaking, your role is to generate sales leads and create opportunities by proactively calling on customers. The valuable skill of creating sales leads results in sales and more business. The ability to create business by creating sales orders is valuable to you and your employer. This ability adds value to a business and defines your role in the purest sense. You're not employed to simply look after the current customer base.

Retaining a customer base is a vital part of business growth. You should always be seeking to add to your base by obtaining new business as this is a better form of business growth. Your goal should be to obtain 80% of your sales orders from new business (people who are not currently customers), while 20% of your sales should be generated from growing and retaining your customer base.

When you become proficient at generating sales leads you will truly be in charge of your own success – not blaming the marketing department or market conditions.

In periods of slow economic growth the inquiry rate is the first thing to drop. Business still continues and potential customers are still out there, but there may be less of them in the market. If you're in the habit of creating business you can still do well in a less prosperous economy by increasing your market share while your competitors wonder where all their enquiries have gone.

To call or not to call?

Let us save you a lot of time and provide some of the common reasons for sales people *not* to cold call:

- It's old-fashioned.
- It's a waste of my time and skill set.
- I'm too busy.
- I don't need to because I'm busy enough.
- I don't need to now that I'm established.
- It's not my job.
- I prefer to relationship sell.
- It's a better use of my time to pursue my contacts and business relationships.

There are plenty more reasons like these. But these excuses should encompass most of the more academic and creative reasons you could think of.

We won't waste time attempting to convince you to engage in some lead generation of your own. Except to say:

Why would you leave lead generation to someone else, thereby passing control of your success to a third party? Why leave it to chance that a referral and lead will come your way? Does it not make sense to want to go to someone and generate as many sales as you can?

Take any risk out of the equation and, despite being helped by lead generation that may be conducted by your company and helped by your marketing department, regardless of your product and brand awareness, it makes sense for you to pursue potential customers.

In sales there can be nothing simpler than this thinking:

"I have a product I want to sell. There is a customer that could or does use what I sell. I'm going to ask them if they want to speak to me. If they don't want to speak to me now, I'll find out when I can see them."

The clarity of this mindset about sales success doesn't need to be explained. Yes, you can also pursue other lead generating activities, such as obtaining referrals, engaging in social media, electronic marketing, sponsorship, attending local business network meetings, or whatever is in vogue this week or appeals to you. But don't disregard the direct simple and foolproof methods of asking someone if they want to sit down and talk to you about what you have to offer, i.e. cold-calling. This approach removes all risk and is quicker than waiting for a lead.

How do we generate leads?

Invariably the same business (potential customer) may be tracked and approached using a variety of contact methods over a period of time. Any type of lead generation activity may prompt a first appointment.

Sales person-initiated marketing action can take the following forms:

- Physical cold call.
- Telephone (telemarketing).
- Mail letter and business card.
- Email.
- Post a flyer or unaddressed mail.

- Attend business networking meetings.
- Post or hand-deliver 3D promotional items.

Many other options are available for contacting customers. Text messages, promotional internet websites, emails with links to internet sites, etc. But let's keep things simple and concentrate on those things a sales person can do very well and be accountable for – talking to people.

Talking to people is the most powerful and customized marketing tool available. More meaning can be conveyed, more information can be gained or shared and it's possibly the safest way to customize a message tone and implied meaning.

A personal discussion is the ultimate tailor-made marketing message. It can be adapted specifically for the target audience in the most personal of ways. Let's not make it any harder than it needs to be – talk to people. When generating leads, don't text, email or use whatever is the next best digital thing. Just talk to people.

The most effective way to do this is by cold-calling in person and telemarketing. This provides you with an opportunity to obtain some feedback about the customer's situation. We'll concentrate on these two major lead generators used by sales people.

A few basics

Whether your lead generation involves cold-calling in person, or using the telephone to call a potential customer, there are a few points to note which are common to both types of prospecting:

- Don't be nervous – be relaxed, be yourself.
- Keep discussions simple and direct.
- Don't feel guilty or be apologetic about interrupting.
- Be positive and upbeat – think "happy go lucky."
- Prospecting is a regular and ongoing part of being successful in a sales job. It must be part of each day or week. It's not something that is only done when you're new to sales, or have a new sales territory to work.

- When you receive a "No", this should be interpreted as "No, not now." It's the wrong time, not the wrong idea!
- In dealing with any rejection understand that the "No's" aren't personal. Find your own way to deal with any negativity you encounter.
- You'll not be successful if the negativity stays with you.
- There's never a perfect time to prospect. Don't create excuses about what is or isn't the appropriate time to prospect. Even Friday afternoon can be an excellent time because most likely your potential customers don't feel like working.
- When prospecting, the aim is not to sell a product or solution outright; it is simply to get to the next stage of the sale, the first appointment.
- It's vital to remind yourself that more calls = more potential customers = more sales = more company profit = more personal income.
- Never tell a potential customer that you're calling to update your database, or because you're the new sales person for their territory. Your reasons for calling should always be about a benefit to your potential customer, not a benefit to you or your company. The reason for your call should be specific to your customer's main points of interest.

Who do we target?

If in doubt, always target the person who "signs the checks," the person authorized to spend the money, or who makes the buying decision. When you successfully contact them they may still direct you to one of their subordinates. This is good, as your new point of contact has been requested to speak to you by their superior. This tends to make discussions move more fluently and deliberately.

You may have legitimate reasons to approach more than one person within an organization. Depending on the size of the company you are calling and the nature of your product, you could be speaking to one or more of these people at any given time:

- Owner.
- Director / President.
- Financial Controller / Accountant.
- Administration Manager.
- IT Manager.
- Purchasing Manager.

If it's practical for you to approach more than one role type, it's likely each person will have their own area of interest. This means you can promote different aspects of your product to each one. For example, the "computer guy" might like to hear about new technology, while the "financial controller" prefers to hear about cost-saving benefits. Tailor your discussion to suit the primary interest of the potential customer you're targeting (obviously this is very product dependent).

Because you probably have multiple contacts you can target, if you fail to obtain a first appointment, based, for example, on a cost-saving analysis with the financial controller, you may have success a week later with the IT manager when you call to arrange an appointment to discuss technology. If that also fails, the office manager may agree to meet with you to discuss the labor-saving aspects of your product.

If we target different contacts and tailor our discussions accordingly, we have a high probability of securing an appointment with that potential customer (organization).

Consider the full applications of your product and try to approach people outside the role type that typically buys your product. The "back door" is often easier to open than the "front door," where everyone tries to get in.

Cold calling – in person
Your first objective is to meet with the person responsible for purchasing the product you sell. If this isn't possible, your next objective is to

establish that person's name and, if possible, find out what product they currently use (that you are seeking to replace).

Some information you may enquire about could include:

- Name of person to contact.
- Title / role of contact person.
- Current product or solution being used.
- Current supplier.
- What they think of their current product or solution.

It's best to ask for a business card or "with compliments" slip as this will have the company address and contact details.

If the contact person does make time to see you, then it essentially turns into a mini-first appointment (see "the first date" questions).

Benefits of prospecting by cold-calling

The benefits of cold-calling will outweigh the fact that compared to other lead generation activity, such as telemarketing, it can be time-consuming. The benefits include:

- The cold-call could turn into a first appointment.
- You may get to see or establish the customer's current product.
- Being able to observe the potential customer helps form an opinion about the type of company they are and how important it is to pursue their business.
- Some potential customers file all the business cards left by sales people and refer to them when they have a need – out of respect for the sales person's effort.
- People are less likely to be dishonest with you in person and, even if they are, you're able to read their body language.
- You put a face to the name and leave the potential customer with a sense of who they're dealing with.

Telemarketing by the sales person

The objective of a telemarketing call is to make a first appointment. When this is not possible the secondary objective is to obtain some information which helps you know when you should follow up with the potential customer.

Telemarketing has a distinct advantage over physical cold-calling. It's more time- effective – a lot of ground can be covered quickly.

The major downside of telemarketing is that you cannot read the situation well. The potential customer may be busy and ignores your call. It's too easy for the potential customer to be dishonest, saying, "We've just upgraded", or "We just bought one," in an effort to terminate the call.

Most sales people have been in appointments with customers where they witness competitor telephone calls being terminated with less than accurate answers.

It pays to be slightly more structured in your work when you engage in telemarketing:

- Ask your colleagues and support people not to interrupt you for a certain period of time so you can concentrate of making outgoing calls.
- Turn your email and cell phone off and concentrate on the task at hand.
- Don't talk to co-workers between calls.
- Smile when you talk.
- Always be polite, but persistent.
- Be clear about your agenda – selling the appointment not the product or solution.
- Once you've obtained an appointment, move to terminate the call and get on to the next one.
- Don't leave a message for the customer as they most probably will not telephone you back. You need to call them again.

Scripts

Some sales people enjoy the security of referring to a "script" when making telephone calls. Scripts can be based around information they already know about the potential customer, or around some generic benefits of their product. Carefully crafted scripts making reference to high profile customers are another common approach and they may have their place in increasing the success rate of setting appointments.

Telemarketing scripts and rehearsed speeches can be effective, but be mindful that customers may be saturated by this. It's of personal preference whether a script yields better results than having a normal discussion with the person on the other end of the telephone.

If telemarketing is about "numbers" (meaning, the more people you call, the more potential customers you can identify) why not be direct and ask if they want to speak to you about your product? Tell them how your product range has helped others and see if they want to talk to you. If you can save someone money or time, directly tell them how without making it into a long speech. Make an appointment and get on to the next call.

Don't make telemarketing out to be a bigger task than it appears.

Do you really think that you're the first person to call from your industry telling them about some exciting changes? How original and sincere is saying "Sorry to bother you, but I have something important you should know about..?"

Before you launch yourself into an hour or two of telemarketing, ask yourself: How different do I sound, compared to the next sales person calling the customer? Do you really think you sound any different, or can you be more inspiring so that you obtain an appointment?

The essence of what you should tell them is this – it's about why you'll not be wasting their time! Doing this quickly and effectively will maximize your results in booking first appointments.

Oh and keep things simple. Confusing people over the phone is unlikely to result in a meeting.

Create the right impression

When you do have an interested person agreeing to make an appointment, don't suggest, "Any time, I'm free that day!" or something similar to this. This doesn't convey to the potential customer that you're a professional who is in demand. Select a time that is convenient and time-effective for you.

Out of hours

If you can't get past the receptionist on the phone, try calling before or after standard business hours. This tends to be effective as management and decision makers usually work longer hours, including when the receptionist isn't there. Calling outside standard hours can be the quickest way past the receptionist, whose role is often designed to block you.

You may find one hour calling out of hours will yield better results than 4 hours calling within standard office hours.

Professional / Full-time prospector

It's common to have hired help to assist in lead generation, for either telephone or cold-call prospecting. This is a perfectly understandable and an appropriate approach if the sales person concentrates on their higher-skilled sales work. With specialization, a better end result may be obtained.

Be mindful that as a sales person you probably take your industry knowledge for granted and often are better placed to create an opportunity and secure an appointment with organizations where the hired help has not been successful. Your experience enables you to pick up on a service, finance or product function issue that the potential customer may discuss. A lead generator may not have sufficient industry knowledge to secure an appointment with the more difficult potential customers.

Liar, liar

There is a high probability when generating leads that you may be provided with information that isn't correct. Many excuses may be used to terminate your cold call or telephone call. Commonly:

- We just bought one.
- Head office does the buying.
- The person responsible is not here.
- We don't have funds in our budget.

You should see excuses for what they are, i.e. another way of saying "It's not convenient to talk right now – we're not interested at present." Don't become demotivated by excuses, or interpret them as a true reflection of the potential customer's circumstances.

Seeing is believing

Nothing can replace being out and about in the field. If you're telemarketing, all companies look the same on the computer screen. A three-person company appears the same as a multi-national organization. Also, if you comb through your sales area diligently you'll locate companies and opportunities that you didn't know existed.

Big opportunities can be missed unless you're actively out and about in the sales territory.

Work your entire sales area. Sales people new to a particular sales territory often unearth potential customers that were previously ignored, or not seen by other sales people. Look through your entire sales territory without prejudice and check every door for opportunity.

It's a habit

You can't leave your prospecting until next week when you think you have more time. Lead generation doesn't work this way. Those perpetually successful sales people understand that it's a fundamental habit to do a little lead generation each and every day. They understand that three cold calls a day will always outweigh two hours of calling planned for next week.

The best day and time to generate leads

Research may suggest particular days and times of the week are more optimal than others to lead generate and this may be true. But any reliance on this kind of research may also be misguided. If the person you're calling at the "right day and time of the week" is not available, the end result is the same.

Any desire to call on the "optimal day in the week" will mostly serve as an excuse to delay any activity until the required day. Any day, any time is the best policy!

Persistence (not stupidity)

Persistence is required in sales because the customer's crystal ball doesn't work any better than our future-predicting crystal ball. Some unexpected circumstance can occur at any time and this could affect the customer's circumstances. You called today and they had no need or desire for your product and maybe viewed your call as a waste of their time. The very next business day something changed (they merged with another company, bought another entity or decided to open a new location or were awarded a tender they didn't anticipate) and they now need what you have to offer.

Persistence, to keep going in the face of the "No's" is what it's all about.

Persistence is to be commended, but not to the extent that you turn off a potential customer from dealing with you when the time is right for them. Balance the frequency and nature of your contact with the potential customer in line with their situation. Rotate as appropriate between e-mail, cold-call in person, telephone calling or sending some product literature. That way you are less likely to upset people.

Don't forget the objective of lead generation

Cold-calling and telemarketing is done to:

- Ascertain if the customer is currently in the market for a product you supply.
- Establish when the customer will next be in the market to buy.

- Obtain an appointment so you can create a need for your product.

The information you record in your database should only be material that contributes to these three objectives. Don't waste time collecting unnecessary details. You're not an information service, you're a sales person employed to sell products or services.

The hidden benefit of cold-calling and telemarketing is not just that you find someone who is in the market for one of your products, but your actions actually create an interest. By proactively calling on potential customers you can create a sale and entice them into the market.

Invariably, looking to address an issue you can solve is something that "they were getting around to." Your call often speeds up the process and encourages customers into the market.

It's lonely

It's lonely out on the road all day. Lots of time spent travelling alone and no-one next to you to talk about the call you just had with the customer.

Try to cold-call in pairs every so often because you're not a machine. Sometimes the loss of productivity is worth it to spend half a day with a colleague, learning from someone else's approach and style.

You don't receive accolades for cold-calling. It's not prestigious or glamorous, but it is a mandatory ingredient to your perpetual success.

The statistic that matters

An Olympic sprinter doesn't look at the clock while they're running. They are focusing on what matters, each step they take. Their time, up on the scoreboard, is the end result of this focus. This is what matters in their success.

The same applies for a football team. Unfortunately, when we're in a sales team people seem to forget this logic. Sales Managers often talk about sales budgets and concentrate on the outcome in discussions with sales people, i.e. they talk about sales achieved. However it is wrong to talk about sales budget numbers, this is looking at the wrong end.

Sales people who ensure that their lead generation activity is always maintained and who value monitoring the number of cold calls and telephone calls, are the people who are measuring what matters. The sales results will follow, as long as the right numbers are going into the top of the sales funnel.

Measuring and monitoring lead generation activity is the only statistic that matters within a sales role.

2.4

The first date

The first appointment

A first appointment is the first opportunity for you to find out about your customer and to tell them a little about yourself.

The customer has an interest, need or possible requirement for one of your products so they have agreed to meet with you. The first appointment is where you're able to establish their need, or you have an opportunity to create a need in their mind.

This is probably the most exciting selling stage. When done correctly, you not only determine what *product* is best to sell to this customer, but more critically you learn *how to sell* to this particular customer. We learn the best way to present our solution to the customer, based on their preference, concerns and emotional view of their current circumstance. We also make note of their opinions about the available options.

80 / 20 Rule

As this is the start of the sales race you must place yourself and your product as a "front runner" in the customer's mind, or you'll be relegated to a sales person who's "just making up the numbers."

In a conversation, the person asking questions is the one in control as they are directing the flow of information. The more information someone has, the greater understanding they'll have of a given situation.

Your main role in a first appointment is to ask as many questions of the customer as possible.

Ideally, in a first appointment the customer should do at least 80% of the talking and you should do 20% at most. While you're talking (unless you're asking a question) you're not learning anything about the customer's situation.

Think of it like this

It may be useful to consider the analogy of a patient visiting a doctor. A patient begins the visit with the complaint they simply describe as "a sore back." Not being able to feel what the patient is referring to the doctor then proceeds to ask a series of more specific questions:

- Where specifically is the pain?
- Is it sore when you stand, when you sit, when you lie down on your back?
- Is the pain consistent all day and all night?
- Is it a constant ache, or a sharp pain felt only during certain movements?
- Have you done any unusual physical activity recently?

With each and every answer the doctor narrows down the possible cause of the pain. The doctor's questions prompt the patient to be more specific about their condition. The more detailed the responses, the greater the information the doctor has to understand the real issue.

Based on the initial, more general responses the doctor receives, she then asks more detailed questions, eventually yielding even more specific information.

It's helpful to note that the doctor doesn't use medical terms. She speaks in the language the patient understands and relates to. She doesn't ask questions such as, "What other symptoms do you have?" As the patient may not know what is meant or implied, the doctor specifically asks questions such as, "Have you experienced any dizzy spells?,"

"Have you experienced any difficulty in breathing?" The patient doesn't know where the doctor is going with all the deliberate questions, but with each question the doctor is able to narrow the issue to a possible cause and identify an appropriate treatment.

A sales person's role in a first appointment is similar to the doctor's approach.

Let the games begin

At the start of the meeting be sure to acknowledge your appreciation of the customer's time and the opportunity provided to meet with them. Then engage in discussions to start building some rapport with the customer.

Often taken out of context by sales people is the need to build rapport on a personal level. It definitely has its place and is binding once a sales person has a personal connection with a customer. It just takes time to achieve.

You should be cautious about discussing your life with the customer. Rapport building at the start of a business relationship is all about the customer. It's about encouraging them to talk to you. So you listen enthusiastically and hear all about their weekend, work, family, or whatever.

It's important to let the customer share their opinion of say, their football team's performance on the weekend, but there's little value in sharing yours. Use the valuable time to get the customer talking and resist the urge to contribute extensively about how you feel about any given topic. The customer cares about *their* opinions, not *yours*. Coincidentally, you're there to care about the customer's opinions, not yours, so it's a good fit!

Don't spoil it by talking about yourself.

Questions, questions, questions

Your questioning is designed to help you better understand two scenarios:

- What the customer currently experiences.
- What the customer wants to experience.

We must ask relevant questions within three main subject areas:

- Product / solution issues (what you are selling).
- Service support (after sale support).
- Payment method issues.

Selling is never solely about the product, although this is a major topic of the discussion. Events may take place after the sale, so your post-sale service and support should be discussed to a certain extent.

Similarly, the acquisition method or the payment terms (how payment will be made) are also likely to be part of the discussion.

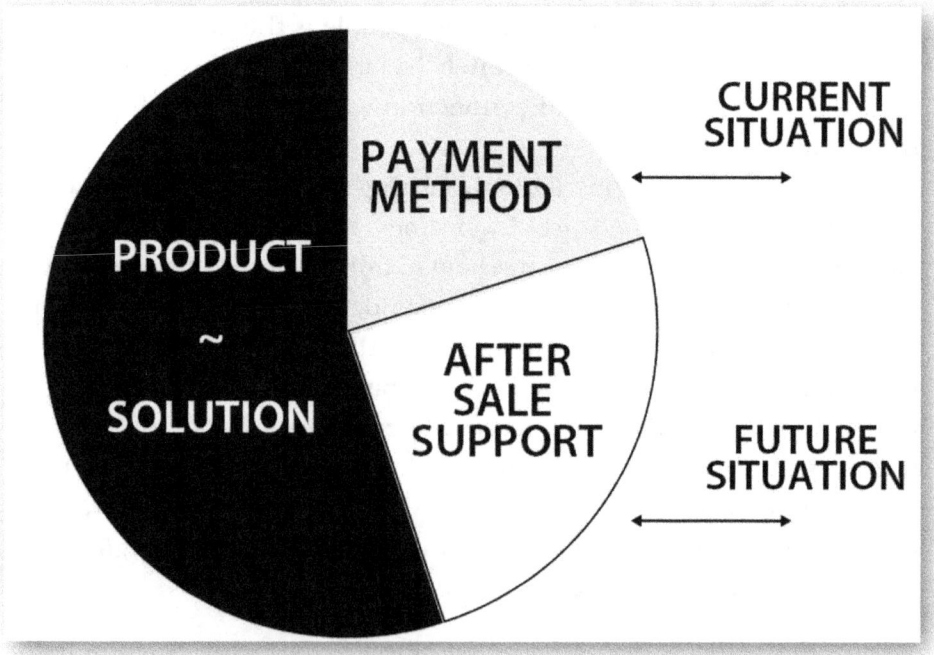

To be thorough we must understand the customer's current situation and experience, as well as their desired future experience – within each of the three areas of product, after-sales service and payment method.

Failing to discuss and understand each of these areas will provide you with only part of the picture.

Even if you had just one product type with no variations that you sell, you would still follow the same process and be asking the customer many questions. This would allow you to understand what's important to them, what they value, what they're looking for and what issues, concerns and frustrations are to be solved.

These are the real reasons we meet to discuss the customer's needs as it tells us how we should present our solutions to them for maximum appeal and impact. By knowing our customer's concerns and frustrations we can tailor our presentations to address their issues without wasting time talking about general "sales points."

If possible it's always easiest to start with questions about the core product you sell, rather than payment methods / terms and service experience issues. Discussing product provides a neutral starting point and gives you an opportunity to feel comfortable speaking to the customer as they already expect your discussions to be about your core product. From that base you can progress on to more complex issues, including service support and payment arrangements.

What if they don't use the product I sell?

At times you may be selling a product the customer has not yet experienced and does not yet use. Your approach should still be similar to what we have outlined.

Obviously you don't ask questions about their product, but you do follow the same thought process and approach. You need to specifically frame your questions about the customer's current method of working that you know your product (which will be new to them) will improve upon.

On one hand it appears easier to sell a product the customer has no preconceived opinion about because they will be more inclined to listen to your sales arguments. However, there is also the possibility that the customer may not initially value the benefits of the product you're proposing because they haven't yet experienced them. In this case it may be a harder sell.

It's a conversation

You should ask questions in a conversational manner, consistent with your personality. It's not an interview or an interrogation! You must be conversational as this will lead to the customer speaking more freely and they'll be less conscious of the extent and depth of your continuous questioning.

Your questions are guided by the nature of the product you supply, but in each of the following categories you should develop a detailed list of questions that you could be asked within your industry. Be sure to encompass all aspects of your solution.

Current situation:

- Product capabilities
- Service and support
- Payment method
- Other factors

Future situation:

- Product capabilities
- Service and support
- Payment method
- Other factors

The questions are designed to give you an understanding of the facts of the matter, as well as determining what your customer thinks of their current and desired situation.

Assume for a moment that you're selling a physical product. Some questions about the customer's current circumstance could be:

Product

- What is the make?
- Which model?
- How old? How long has it been in use?
- What other, similar products are in use elsewhere in the organization?
- What's good about the product?
- What can be improved about the product?
- Has the product performed reliably?
- Why are you changing the product?

Service and support

- Who is your current service supplier?
- Have they supported the product since installation?
- What level of service have you received?
- What was the typical response to an enquiry?
- How would you rate the overall reliability of the product?
- Has the service been expensive?
- What are your current service costs?
- Is this amount tax-inclusive or tax-exclusive?
- What does it include?
- What was not included in your after-sales service costs?
- Are there any extra costs for supporting the product?
- Is there a service contract in place?
- When does the service agreement expire?
- Is there a fee or penalty for terminating the service agreement?
- How has the cost for service changed since the agreement started?

Finance / Payment method

- What payment method was used?
- Do you pay on credit terms?
- Is there a payout on the current agreement?
- Do you own the product at the expiry of the finance agreement?
- How have the costs changed since the start of the agreement?
- Are there any other items of equipment in the finance agreement?

Other factors

Most times there are other factors not automatically identified by the customer as being relevant to the discussions. However the sales person is alert to factors which may be related to their solution. Invariably, questions will need to be asked to uncover any indirect needs, as the customer is unlikely to divulge this information automatically.

Questions could be:

- Do you have any additional sites where you have similar products in use?
- What products do you use there?
- Are there any factors not discussed that are driving this replacement?
- Does the future direction of the organization influence what product requirements you currently have?

Other factors will be driven by the nature of your product and will tend to be product-specific.

Having addressed the current circumstance, similar questions should be used to understand the customer's future circumstances. What does the customer want to achieve moving forward?

Get the full picture

Having established the customer's current situation and future requirements we can ask more general questions to help us better understand the sale. For example:

- What is the approval system to facilitate placing an order?
- When do you need to take delivery/commence?
- What are the timeframes for making a decision?
- What stage are you at in terms of buying?
- Have you seen others?
- What suppliers are you considering?
- What other product models are you considering?
- How much are they?
- What is their product cost?
- What is their service cost?
- What do you like about their options?
- What concerns you about their options?
- In making a change, what are the logistics to implement a new product?
- What are the logistics to implement a new supplier?

Ask these types of questions towards the end of your appointment. At this stage, you should have built a level of trust as a result of your thoroughness and attention to detail. The answers to these questions help you understand the sale better and let you know how you need to go about things in relation to your competitors.

Be logical

Better results are achieved if you complete your questions within each topic area before discussing the next area of interest. Naturally this isn't always possible, given the nature of discussions, but you should attempt to be logical in your discussion, not jumping from topic to topic, as you'll have limited time to establish the situation.

Questions about the customer's future situation often encroach on their business plans and future direction. This can be sensitive information, so leading with these types of questions isn't a great idea; wait until the customer is more at ease and is starting to trust you.

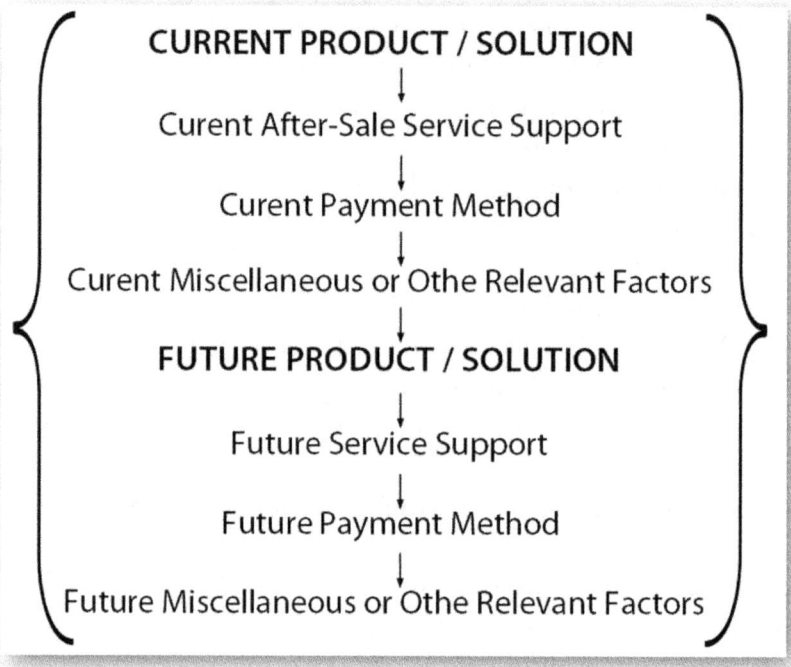

Get them talking

Obviously, asking questions that can only be answered with a "yes" or "no" will not lead to informative conversation. Some examples of "conversation starters" that tend to lead to discussion are provided below:

- You look very busy, what's your role?
- Have you been happy with the service provided by your current supplier?

- How has your current supplier given you good value for money?
- What is your perception of our industry?
- Are you familiar with our industry?
- Have you bought a (product name) before? So you know what a "soap opera" it can be?
- I know you're busy and I don't want to waste your time, but how realistic is it that you'll leave your current supplier?
- I assume from your perspective that it's possibly a case of "you're safer with the devil you know than the one you don't"?
- What factors will influence your ultimate decision the most?
- When you decide to select a supplier, how are you going to judge which option provides you with the best value for money? Is it simply a matter of selecting the lowest price option?
- How do you define "value for money" when making your decision?

The more experience you gain, the more confident you'll feel about asking these types of questions – they tend to elicit more informative responses.

Remember that the more open-ended questions you ask (those that cannot be answered with a "yes" or "no" response) the better chance there is of the customer revealing their true concerns and needs. This information is key to being able to provide a customized, meaningful sales presentation and solution.

Assume nothing

Asking questions over many appointments makes it easy to miss the answer because you become conditioned to expecting the same or similar responses.

Never assume that you know what your customer is about to say. Force yourself to listen as you'll be surprised by some people's viewpoints. If you pick up one or more important issues that your competitors missed, it may make the difference between securing and losing the sales order.

If you don't understand an answer to one of your questions, or don't fully appreciate the answer, don't assume you know why the customer is saying something. Ask for clarification. This will help you get to the reasons why the customer thinks as they do.

Did we mention persistence?

Yes, we already have. But let's "persist" some more.

It's rare to have a customer that doesn't want to talk about what they want, or won't talk in detail if you ask questions. Occasionally you may be faced with a customer that appears tough and is clearly "anti-sales person". This can be quickly overcome with relaxed persistence.

To instigate a conversation with "unfriendly" customers, begin your sales presentation using sales tools or documents and slowly start to ask questions in a conversational manner. It won't feel like interrogation to the customer and you'll establish all that you need to know. Sometimes you need to start the discussions with a generic sales presentation, but as soon as you can, switch to asking your questions.

Third time lucky

Some customers are initially guarded about the information they provide and they won't reveal specifics. Always persist and ask the same questions in three different ways. Never give up, until you've failed three times. You'll be amazed at the result.

For example, you may wish to establish what the customer pays per month for their current product. You could ask:

- "How much is the current rental?"
- "Is it expensive?"
- "What do you pay per month?"
- "Do you pay much?"
- "Is it a fixed monthly amount, or does it vary?"
- "Has your monthly rental amount changed much over the period that you've had the machine?"

- "What are you paying now?"
- "Is your current machine good value for money? What do you pay?"

You may know that monthly rental amounts are always fixed, but these questions simply seek to start discussions about the monthly payment amount. Just don't ask all of these questions one after another!

When appropriate, incorporate some of these questions during your discussions. The added benefit of casually asking, "Is it expensive?" is that you not only establish what they currently pay, but also establish what the customer thinks is expensive or cheap.

Listen!

People who listen earn greater trust. The more you listen, the more the customer likes you and rapport is built.

Think about your personal circumstances. Are those people you trust more likely to be the people who talk most or talk the least? It's always easier to impress someone by being interested in them and in what they have to say, as opposed to talking at them in an effort to impress them.

You'll be surprised what people tell you if you:

1. Ask a question.
2. Wait for them to answer it.
3. Actually listen to their answer.

As you do this every day you invariably know what the end result of your questioning will be. You'll very quickly have a good idea as to what the customer needs and what product you should sell to them. But you should still be patient and listen to what they have to say. You're asking questions of the customer and in doing so you're getting them to really think about their situation, including what they're looking to achieve and what they're already doing.

We're getting the customer to ask these questions in their own mind, in their own words. This is a valuable component of what we're doing as they'll always listen to themselves more than they'll listen to you. Take the time to ask questions, listen to the answers and lead them through the process, letting them use their own thoughts and words to decide that you are the best option for them.

Armed with your industry knowledge you need to do the customer's thinking for them by prompting them with questions that encourage them to assess the full picture. You do this every day, but always remember that the customer does not. Be patient, as in effect, you're doing the customer's thinking for them.

It's pointless working in this manner without actively listening to the information you have solicited. Know the reason why you ask so many questions, ask questions that matter and ensure you listen attentively to the customer.

Why, why, why?

Asking a question and obtaining the customer's answer is important. But understanding why they're answering in a particular way will often provide valuable information as you work your way through the steps of the sale.

In a sense, as a sales person you want to try to get behind the answer by understanding the cause or real issues. This will help you address the customer's real pain. Asking "Why?" in response to answers provided by the customer will quickly lead you to grasping their true situation. More experienced sales people will do this with greater ease and see it as a standard part of their approach.

You'll be surprised how asking "Why?" and doing so often, will result in greater information being shared by the customer.

Create concerns

We ask questions to uncover the customer's needs (which we subsequently solve). By encouraging the customer to think about details we are educating them to think about all the variables they should be considering.

Many of our questions, along with parts of our sales presentation, will raise a concern that the customer hadn't previously thought of. Naturally, the questions and issues you emphasize (the areas of concern you highlight) should relate to your competitive advantages, i.e. relate to the problems your product can solve. There are many areas of concern you could raise that are addressed by your product or supply method.

Often it may be a series of small points, not a mainstream sales argument that you use to educate the customer about the safety of selecting your solution. For example:

"Our automatic billing system ensures that you're automatically invoiced correctly, without human intervention and we don't charge you a minimum amount; you're only invoiced for what you consume."

By advising the customer how your company operates in a fair and equitable manner you may imply that other companies in this industry have a different practice. The sales person "scores a few points" in the customer's mind because of the thoroughness and attention to detail that they're conveying (issues the customer hadn't thought of) and the assumption that your company's practice is superior to the competitors (especially since the competitor didn't raise this topic in their discussions).

Keep them on track
If your customer talks "off topic" for too long at any stage during your fact find, ask them questions to bring them back on topic. If they love talking so much, you may as well find out everything you need to know before you run out of time.

Take notes
Ensure that you have a folder, notebook and pen with you as you discuss the issues with your customer. You may even choose to have a checklist

of questions to help prompt you (though it may be better not to display it). Take your time to write notes about what the customer is telling you, as this will:

- Help you plan a tailored and relevant demonstration and proposal.
- Reassure the customer that what they're saying is important to you.
- Differentiate you as a professional, setting you apart from your competitors.

It's often valuable to make a few more notes straight after the appointment so relevant details are not forgotten. At the end of a busy day it's hard to remember which customer said what.

It's show time!

Having asked many questions you should now understand which of your products is best to demonstrate and propose. You should also now understand some of the concerns and important issues in the customer's mind.

Equipped with this knowledge, it's now time to give the customer tailored (not general) information as to why your solution is the most appropriate for them. While it may be tempting to try this during the fact finding phase, your delivery will be more powerful if you wait until the questioning phase is over before presenting your solution.

This is the time where you move from appearing to be passive about what is happening to appearing to be passionate about what you have to offer. Your tempo must move up a gear as this is the start of "show time."

Start to show & tell

Regardless of how well-presented you are and how well you listen or communicate, be aware that in a distant corner of the customer's mind they probably still see you as a "sales person". And with this comes all the usual connotations associated with a typical sales person. You therefore need to work hard to overcome this basic stereotype.

In addition to what you say, you may find some sort of visual aids that explain what you're talking about help to focus the customer's attention. The aids also help to reinforce your level of preparation and professionalism. It's easier to capture the customer's imagination with images and presentation tools. They can be hard copy documents, electronic displays or samples of product. Use them to demonstrate a point as it's more believable to the customer when "proof" is automatically provided as part of the discussion.

Get excited

When presenting your solution you must be confident, upbeat and enthusiastic about what you have to offer. Get excited!

The better your delivery, the more engaged the customer becomes. Reveal your passion for your solution as it's not only contagious, but reassures the customer that they're dealing with the right person.

Ask more questions

It's important to ensure that your sales argument delivery is not a monologue. Even though it's your turn to talk and to impress the customer, you should punctuate your presentation with questions to keep them engaged. Some "questions" might include:

- Does that make sense?
- Do you have a need for that in your organization?
- Is that important to you?
- Does that have relevance?

Not only are you keeping the customer engaged, but they'll be giving you more information about what they want and what's important to them.

One solution at a time

Solve one problem at a time. Don't confuse the customer. Clearly outline the solution to each issue raised in your earlier discussion and ensure that it's clear in the customer's mind before you move on to the next issue.

Deliver only one "sales advantage" at a time to ensure it is heard, understood and retained by the customer.

Attention to detail

When you're discussing your mainstream sales stories during a first appointment it is the attention to detail and relevance of that detail that will keep the customer engaged.

For example, we don't say:

"Our response time to your product fault calls is between 4 and 8 hours."

On face value this seems to be an appropriate sales argument, but it's better to say:

"All sales people will tell you that their average response time to fault calls is between 4 and 8 hours. Be mindful that the reliability of your machine is not a function of the speed a technical service engineer can attend your premises, especially if they don't know what to do when they get there. The reliability of your machine is a function of:

- Technology within the product
- Accessibility of spare parts and components
- Quality of spare parts used by the supplier
- Number of field technicians trained on your product type
- Speed and efficiency of service control department
- Any preventative maintenance service system."

Once we have these more detailed discussions with our customers they tend to relax and are more honest with us. Customers enjoy talking to sales people who know all about their solution.

Current customer appointment

If you have a scheduled appointment with a current customer, ensure that you have all the relevant information that you need.

Know your customer's details. You're only one small part of their business. They won't recall the specifics of their purchases and agreements with you. By having this knowledge and being organized it will convey a sense of confidence in dealing with you which leads to them continuing to do business with you.

During your appointment, be sure to specifically ask if the customer has any current or future needs for any of your products. You need to specifically name the other product types that you sell. The customer will not remember all that you offer.

To sum up – more questions

Once you've finished your presentation seek feedback from the customer, again in a manner that's in keeping with your experience, confidence and personality.

You could make comments like:

- Do you have any questions or concerns about our company?
- Is there anything I have said that concerns you?
- Is there anything you heard that you don't quite believe or thought sounded like a sales pitch?
- Have you heard of any other products that sounded more appealing? Chances are our solution can also help – we just haven't discussed it yet!
- There is so much to talk about and trying to cover the product, our service support and payment options in a limited time is difficult. If someone else suggests something more appealing please give me a call and I'll clarify things for you.
- I know there's a lot to remember and this makes it hard for you to pass on to your colleagues. If you'd like me to discuss our solution with others I'm more than happy to do so.

Responses to these general statements and questions provide further information that helps you understand where you're positioned
compared to your competitors. This way you'll know how to plan your
next step.

Confirm the next step

The final part of a first appointment is to be clear about and agree the
timing and intention of the next step. This will be different for all customers. You may need to make another appointment or organize a demonstration, but ensure you agree on the timing and nature of your next
contact before you leave.

2.5

Entertain me

Demonstrating your product or service

It may seem "over the top" to talk in terms of demonstrating some products, but a demonstration is a great way to impress your customer. It's not about you talking; it's about getting your customer to touch, feel, experience and understand the benefits of your product.

See this step as "putting on a show" for your customer as it's here that you want to impress them beyond their expectations. In fact, look at this as an opportunity to entertain them. Always remember that, at the end of the day, all business is "show business."

This stage is often avoided by sales people, sometimes because they're fundamentally lazy, but more commonly because they don't appreciate the need for it.

Whether you encourage customers to partake in a demonstration may be a function of the reputation and market share your company enjoys. If the customer doesn't know you it makes sense to take the time to demonstrate what you're offering. If they know all about you and are content with this it may not be mandatory to demonstrate.

Making a decision about a demonstration might also depend on the value of the product you're selling. The higher the expenditure the greater the chance the customer will ask for a demonstration, rather than needing to be convinced to have one. Either way, it's a great way to set yourself apart as it puts the customer at ease about the decision they're making. That's because they're no longer stepping into the unknown. They've seen it for themselves.

Emotions

By inviting your customer to touch, feel and experience your product or service offering it provides a comfort and puts them at ease for the decision they're about to make. As we said earlier, if done well, your demonstration should take it to the next level and entertain the customer. It's a show you're putting on and if you impress them above their expectations their emotional desire to work with you – and buy from you – will be hard for your competitors to beat.

Mandatory demonstrations

If several competitors are chasing the sale, your selling price is higher than others, or you're not the dominant supplier in your market, a demonstration should be mandatory. Presenting a well-crafted demonstration will ensure you create a good competitive advantage.

The demonstration should be conducted before you present your proposal. Think about how you can establish the expectation in the first appointment that it's common practice for the customer to assess your product via a demonstration before they can be confident about what you're promising.

Rehearse the show

You must be confident, knowledgeable, calm and fluent when you're displaying your product or solution. The ability to do this doesn't happen overnight!

To be knowledgeable and fluent you need to practice, practice and practice again. It's probably more appropriate to say, "Rehearse, rehearse and rehearse again". You can't afford to send the wrong message to the customer if you make a mistake during your demonstration. You need to get it right.

It's show and tell, not tell

The demonstration is not about telling your prospect that you're the best. It's about you showing them why your product is the best. You must understand the difference between "show" and "tell".

During the demonstration

At the commencement of your meeting and before you begin the demonstration, ask if anything has changed since you last spoke. If things have changed, this may alter the structure of your demonstration.

What you demonstrate and the order of the features and benefits that you demonstrate will be driven by what you know about the customer's needs.

Always demonstrate in the order that you know the customer is most interested in.

As you demonstrate you must also take the opportunity to present your sales story. It's a repetition of what you may have previously discussed. Don't assume the customer remembers everything you've previously told them. The demonstration is an opportunity to "display" sales arguments which you've previously discussed. Don't feel as if you are unnecessarily repeating yourself.

Where to demonstrate

A demonstration can take many forms and happen in different locations. Examples include:

- Customer attends your showroom.
- Customer has a trial use of the product.
- Customer attends an existing customer's premises to observe your product or service in use.
- Practical presentation in customer's premises.

In the event you are demonstrating your product in the customer's premises and some technical calibration or set-up is required, ensure that you're fully prepared. Organize the required details by working with the decision maker's subordinates so you don't waste the decision maker's time. Delays in setting up, or an incorrect execution of your demonstration won't be looked upon favorably.

It's not about the product

Your demonstration should display the advantages and benefits of your product. More importantly, it should be a time where you demonstrate your *solution* to the customer along with your appropriateness as a supplier.

Demonstrating "the company", as opposed to "the product" will yield superior results.

You should attempt to demonstrate the systems and, if possible, some of the people involved in the delivery of the product or service support. This is a more powerful sales story.

You may wish to display your "back office" operations to customers in an effort to convey the business culture that exists. You could show your customer:

- Warehouse stock of parts and consumables.
- Service control department and the systems in use.
- Company workshop.
- Technical service engineer's training facilities.
- Quality assurance systems.
- Customer service systems.

If the demonstration takes place at your premises you can invite other, non-sales staff, to your presentation. If your customer hears from, for example, your Service Manager, or an administration staff member about a system or process, and this validates what you have told your customer in a previous meeting, it sends a very powerful message to the customer.

Always be mindful that from the customer's perspective, one word from a staff member not involved in the sales department is more effective than a thousand words from a sales person!

Of course, a demonstration of your back office may not be possible or practical for some suppliers and products. But these demonstrations can't be easily compared to or replicated by your competitors.

2.6

The proposal

The proposal is written proof that you listened to the customer. It's your proposition about how you're going to be good for them. It should outline the solutions to all the problems, issues and concerns that you've identified. It should also outline all the relevant benefits your product will provide to this customer.

Before presenting a written proposal, be sure to ask if anything has changed since you last spoke. The customer's response may affect the way you present or how you might emphasize aspects of the written proposal.

If your customer requires you to supply a low value product you shouldn't waste time preparing and presenting a written proposal. Let common sense prevail.

Rarely is it appropriate to provide your proposal electronically without meeting with the customer. You should always present your hard-copy proposal in person as this creates another opportunity for you to sell to the customer. By taking the customer through the proposal you have an opportunity to assess their body language, view their response and address any concerns or objections they may have.

Computer-generated document templates can greatly assist with the quick preparation of each proposal. However, be sure to personalize each one, emphasizing details that are important to particular customers. You should also present your proposal details in order of importance – the order that is important to the customer.

Pick your time

Only present proposals when the customer is actually in the market. If you know that the decision is not being made for another four weeks or six months, organize to present a proposal closer to decision time.

This approach has distinct advantages. Firstly, things can change and you'll not have the opportunity to present your information twice – you don't want a customer to make a decision based on old information. The second strategic advantage of presenting closer to decision time is that you'll be aware when the decision is being made. If they've had your proposal for months the decision may be made without your awareness or involvement.

The proposal may do the selling for you when you're not there. All details outlined in the proposal must be relevant to the customer. There's no point including details that have no relevance or benefit. Don't use industry jargon or abbreviations that the customer may not understand. The contents should be relevant and thorough, but it should be easy to understand, i.e. anyone outside of your industry should be able to understand your proposal without having been part of the sales process.

Provide a solution, not options

The proposal documents your solution to the customer's requirements. If you're proposing more than one solution with a variety of options you haven't done your job.

For starters, you haven't questioned the customer sufficiently. You shouldn't expect them to place a sales order with you as you don't have control in the selling situation. Essentially, you should be telling the customer what they must do, based on their current situation. If you're unable to do this you won't have control of the sale and you shouldn't expect to win the sales order.

Don't add "extras"

Avoid the temptation to include additional information "just in case." This is not an exercise in customer service. For example, if the potential customer will be acquiring the solution under a pay-by-installment plan, don't include an outright capital purchase price (unless local legislation requires you to do so). Such "extra" information may confuse the customer or create new concerns and objections. If the customer requires extra information they will ask you. This will also tell you that a decision is being made so you can stay in close contact.

Provide the right amount of information

Written proposals often run the risk of either being too vague or too detailed. Providing the right amount of information means different things for different customers. If a customer is considering one product of value it may require a proposal with a maximum of say, six pages. Conversely, a customer looking to purchase 1000 of your high-value products may require a more in-depth document.

It's not always the size of the potential order that determines the length and depth of a proposal, but the nature and outlook of your customer. Do what's best for each sale and avoid generic proposals – one size doesn't fit all.

The format and structure of the written proposal is obviously personal preference and industry-specific. Regardless of the structure, it should clearly:

- Identify the customer issues.
- Demonstrate how your product will address these concerns.
- Clearly outline the payment required.
- Promote additional generic benefits the customer may value.
- Provide a brief comparison between the customer's current and proposed financial expenditure.

The bottom line

A financial comparison page compares the customer's current expenditure to that of your proposed solution. This page is often neglected as the sales person doesn't obtain enough details about the customer's current expenditure. This comparison is really useful from a selling perspective because in effect, you're doing the customer's job for them.

Use the proposal in your discussion
When presenting proposals:

- Always present it in person.
- Step the customer through all the pertinent information.
- Discuss and recap all the important points. Don't assume the customer remembers everything you've previously spoken about.
- Use your pen to direct the customer's eye as you discuss certain aspects of the proposal.
- Watch for the customer's immediate reaction when you talk about the price.
- Once complete, ask the customer what they think. Ask how it compares.
- Don't avoid any costs, fees or fine print. If you don't talk about these details your competitor will tell the customer what they missed in your proposal.

Before leaving the appointment, be sure to ascertain what and when the next step will be. You need to know the customer's next move and timing. Agree a plan with the customer as to when you'll contact them to follow up. This will be their opportunity to ask further questions, having reviewed the proposal in their own time.

Current customer proposals
When preparing a written proposal for an existing customer – because you are selling them additional or replacement products – include statistics and details about your past service performance. Detail what you've already done for them. This may be time-consuming, but it's worth the effort. It's helpful to acknowledge what you have done for them in the past as they may be too busy to appreciate this.

Similarly, customers will tend to take your service level for granted and may assume it to be "standard" for all suppliers. They too are busy and may not realize what you have done. Remind them by presenting the facts and don't assume they know or favor your new product offering.

2.7

Let's talk

Negotiating – bring on the objections

When you're given the opportunity to sell your product and you follow the steps of the sale (stages of the selling cycle), you'll find the customer has few objections in relation to agreeing to purchase your product.

It's important to remember that a "negotiation" is simply a matter of discussing any issues your customer may have with your proposal and clarifying those issues. There's no need to view it in any other way. It's a discussion, not a conflict.

A customer could have concerns or questions in their mind preventing them from proceeding. These concerns could relate to:

- The product.
- After sale service support.
- Price or payment terms.

As a sales person you want objections!

Objections raised by the customer shouldn't be feared. We want to hear their concerns. If we don't know about concerns or perceived shortcomings of our product, then we miss the opportunity to clarify or justify these for the customer.

Be proactive

Anticipate any common objections or questions you think a customer may have, based on your experience. Proactively build answers and explanations into your sales presentations to address them. You'll probably answer many of the customer's concerns or issues before they think of them!

It's always worth thinking about your proposed solution from the customer's viewpoint. This way you can spot any potential objections and deal with them before the customer contemplates them.

Listen first

When the customer outlines their objections or concerns, it's important that you let them finish before you answer. You may have heard the questions many times before, or you may have a perfect reply that instantly removes the objection, but be patient. Listen to the customer fully, clarify what the real issue is and then explain the solution. Don't be over-eager.

Silence is OK

When negotiating, silence is okay. You don't need to fill any pauses with the sound of your voice. This is not only wasted effort, but it makes you look like a "typical" sales person. If responding, make your point and then stop talking. Don't talk too much; if the customer is deep in thought, don't interrupt. Learn to wait.

Never guess the answer

If a customer asks a question or voices an objection that you don't have a solution for, seek clarification or further explanation. Ask them the reason for their question as this will give you time to think of an appropriate response.

If you don't know an answer to a customer's question, say so and tell them when you'll get back to them with the answer. Never guess.

If your solution can't do something, be honest with the customer, but also explain why you're unable to accommodate their request.

Answer with a "Yes"

Always answer in the positive. It's better for the customer to hear a series of "Yes" responses as opposed to "No's."

For example, if the customer asks, "Is your monthly service fee fixed?" Which answer sounds better?

"No, we alter the price every year over the life of the service agreement." OR

"Yes, it is fixed for 12 months from the commencement date and it will be reviewed annually."

Get the facts

When the customer refers to "competitive quotes" from others, suggest that you compare solutions for them. Take your customer through your competitor's quote and help them understand it. Discuss what it does and doesn't say.

This way you'll be comparing facts, not perceptions. Your competition may make some claims your customer likes, but they may not realize you can provide the same benefits. You'll know your industry better than the customer so you'll know what to look for when comparing quotes.

Use customer-friendly terms

When explaining concepts or negotiating, it may be appropriate to draw analogies within the customer's industry. The customer will understand their industry and be able to relate to the issues of price, service and quality in the context of their business.

Avoid making analogies with generic industries as many sales people do this and you don't want to be like "most" sales people. Draw an analogy with the customer's industry as they can better relate to that.

Put things in perspective

Sometimes a customer can be misled by a sales competitor who is promoting a feature or service which is unique to their product. If you can't provide that feature or service, bring the customer back to reality and ask, "How often would you use that?" "How important is it in your current business to be able to do that?"

Invariably, once you get the customer to consider the reality of their workflow, it may no longer be a big issue, nor an advantage to your competitor.

Explain the differences

If asked by a customer, always have a plausible reason as to why you don't do what your competitors do. Don't apologize for what you can't do. Tell them why you operate in this way.

For example, a customer asks: "Can you deliver your product this week? Your competitors can deliver tomorrow?"

A possible response could be:

"We take nine working days to deliver, from receipt of your signed order. The reason for this timeframe is due to the popularity of our product and our internal quality control procedures. All of our new products are tested thoroughly before delivery and installation. We'd like to deliver tomorrow, but we can't compromise our quality process."

These types of answers turn the negative of what you can't do into a positive.

Two sides to every story

Every sales argument has an opposite sales argument which, if presented consistently throughout the steps of the sale, is equally plausible and attractive to a customer. For example, one supplier may be a nation-wide company and have a centralized service support center to provide after sale support. Another supplier may have only one small office in the same town as the customer. Which sales argument is better?

Supplier 1: National call center – thirty telephone operators taking calls.

Sales arguments used by the sales person:

- Always have staff available to take your call.
- Fully-computerized system to receive and log calls and dispatch technical service engineers.
- Phone line available ten hours a day.
- Service unaffected by staff absenteeism due to amount of staff available.
- Automatic phone answer to speed up and direct your call.

Supplier 2: Local service control center – two telephone operators taking calls.

Sales arguments used by the sales person:

- Only need your company name when you call, don't require a customer or product number.
- Operators become familiar with customers as they always deal with the same people each time.
- The operator's knowledge of your geographical area allows the service controller to provide a realistic idea of a technical support engineer's arrival time at customer's premises.
- The customer won't get lost in the system, because of personalized service.
- No long waiting periods for calls to be taken as ratio of customers to service staff is lower than national competitor.
- No computerized answering service, you're able to speak to real people.

Can you see how it's possible to make a service control center with only two telephone operators look more appealing than one with thirty service controllers?

Handling price objections

The ability to handle a direct objection to the price you've proposed means you can maintain a good profit or sales margin. Put simply, if we follow the steps of the sale and perform better in each stage, we are better able to justify a higher price than our competitors.

When the objection of "your price is too high" is raised, you need to be able to work through the objection without feeling the need to match someone else's price. This is a valuable – and profitable – skill. It's pointless getting this far in a potential sale after working diligently for so long, only to give away acceptable profit and sales margin in pursuit of a sales order. Leave desperation to your competitors!

Only engage in price discussions with your customer if they are ready, willing and able to make a decision to place a sales order. Any price-related negotiations prior to this time are pointless and a waste of time.

Typically, customers will only voice concerns over price when you've won or are close to winning the sale. There's little point in the customer talking about price with you if they don't want what you're offering.

When the customer asks for a "better deal" do not make them feel stupid for asking. In your own style, acknowledge that you understand why they are asking, then explain that if you could have sold it for less than the proposed amount you would have done so.

Be concise

The key to this is to explain your reasons concisely without going on about it.

For example, you might say that you didn't want to waste their time by attempting to charge them more than what was required. Alternately, you could tell the customer that given the quality of your product you don't have the luxury to charge higher prices as there are many cheaper, low-quality products available in your market.

Similarly, you could say something to effect of: "I would love to be able to lower my price for you and it would certainly make my job easier, but given the quality of our product it's just not possible."

Select whichever approach works best for you and your personality, but firstly acknowledge the validity of the customer's request for a discounted price.

You can see how your approach to handling price-specific discussions is consistent with your general approach throughout the sales process, i.e. maintaining quality and attention to detail.

Don't adopt the mindset of, "Well if I match that price will you give me an order?" or "If I ask my Sales Manager to discount then can we proceed with the order?" We don't approach a potential sale with the view that in order to get it we must give something away first. Our mindset is, "Yes, we understand why you ask for a discount, we'd like to accommodate you, but we have some realities to contend with."

Don't forget that, generally speaking, a customer is having this discussion with you because they want to deal with you and your solution. You have gained number one preference because of how you went about your job, outlining your product, service support and payment methods. Therefore you must capitalize on the effort you've already expended and don't falter at this stage. This applies even if your competitors are selling the same product.

Follow a process

Here's an example of how you should handle a price objection. Follow this approach and the results will be self-evident (follow the steps outlined by A to D)

Customer: "You're out on price, you're too expensive."

A. Sales Person: "Compared to what?"
Don't say more than this! Just politely wait for the answer.

The customer's answer will indicate who your nearest competitor is. If the customer is vague then you know that they may not be sincere about "others being cheaper". In fact, they may be ready to make a decision now and price is not really the issue.

If your product has multi-faceted pricing, such as payment for a product and a separate payment for after sales services, clarify the issue with the customer. Ask them if the price issue pertains to payment for the product or service support. Importantly, listen to their answer, acknowledge that answer and leave it at this. Don't pursue a detailed discussion. Continue by asking the following question:

B. <u>Sales Person</u>:   "If all prices were equal, which supplier would you select?"

Regardless of the customer's answer, just ask the following without distraction or additional comment:

C. <u>Sales Person</u>:   "Why?"

Now the customer is telling you about which supplier and solution they prefer and the reasons why. Continue on and encourage them to more fully explain their reason by asking the following type of question:

D. <u>Sales Person</u>:   "Why is this important to you?" OR
"Why is that good for you?"

In answering these questions the customer has told you what advantages or benefits they see in their preferred solution. They have told you which option they believe they should select and why.

Obviously, they may have just explained why they want your solution, or why they want your competitor's solution.

If they've outlined your competitor as their preferred option you now know that the *real* reason for their objection wasn't the price.

Your next step is to address all the issues that you've just heard and compare them to your solution. Often you'll also be able to provide what it is that your competitor is offering, but the customer may have missed this fact. You've not lost this sale; you just have more work to do!

If the customer outlined why they want to go with your solution then you have won the battle in the customer's mind and you now need to justify why the price is what it is. You now need to "sell" the difference in price between your solution and the competitor to which you are being compared. You don't need to justify your price; you need to justify the price *difference*.

This should not be viewed as a hard task as the customer has just told you why you are better than your competitor.

The above process may sound a little too simple or academic to work in the real world. But by using your own conversational style and following the above steps (A to D), without deviation and distraction, you'll be amazed how effective it is and what the customer tells you.

Justifying the price difference

When you're negotiating on price, present the numbers in the best possible way to maximize the impact on the customer. Have a calculator with you and do the calculation, together with the customer. Customers will believe a calculator before they believe a sales person!

Naturally this may vary with product type, but when discussing price and the impact it may have on a business it's appropriate to take the difference in pricing between your proposed price and that of your nearest competitor and express the price difference as a weekly amount.

For example, if your product is sold in say, monthly installment amounts and the amount that you offered was $80 per month more than your competitor, discuss it in terms of a difference of $18 a week. You may even ask your customer if spending $3.60 a day more on your product is worth it, given the security and peace of mind that your solution offers.

This has been calculated as follows:
 $80 x 12 months = $960
 52 weeks in a year
 $960 / 52 weeks
 $18.46 per week extra

Asking for an extra $18 per week sounds better than asking for $80 per month, or $960 per year.

A similar process can be taken if the payment required is a large lump sum. For example, let's say you're $ 80 000 more expensive than your nearest competitor and your solution has a 3-year lifespan. Talking about an additional $ 2 300 per month sounds better than asking for an additional $ 80 000.

This has been calculated as follows:
 $ 80 000 / 36 months = $ 2 223 a month.

If tax is required to be added it's also helpful to talk about the cost to the customer as being the amount "plus tax." This way you'll be discussing smaller numbers and the tax component is consistent for all suppliers.

The majority of customers don't expect sales people to have these kinds of discussions. Using this tactic will more often than not remove the need to discount. At times, customers will be apologetic about asking the pricing question, confessing that they "just had to ask anyway."

Strange questions

If you're at the end of the selling cycle be sure to take note if your customer starts asking pedantic questions or questions that you thought you'd already answered. These can be questions that appear unrelated to the core issues you've previously discussed. Suddenly the customer is asking about some aspect that was not a factor previously.

This scenario suggests that you may be losing control. Most probably, a competitor is attempting to portray some feature as an important advantage. These, out of the blue questions can be a signal that your competitor may have the ear of your customer. This means you've still got some work to do.

Beware the incentives

Most negotiations will take place around price or sales incentives (incentives to buy). Commonly, your customer doesn't stop to ask you for a discount, or for sales giveaways. It usually occurs as a result of your competitor's actions, when they can see that the customer is not favoring them. The customer turns to you to see what you can also offer them.

Sales incentives and offers are packaged in many forms, accompanied with all sorts of justifications. From additional and free products to handsome discounts of initial prices quoted. The list is endless.

How do you handle competitor giveaways and sales incentives?

Your first option is to join them and also give away products and services. This doesn't build a competitive advantage as you'll be making your solution look similar to that of your competitor. Obviously our objective is the opposite, so matching a giveaway is neither viable, nor a commercially sensible option.

When asked by your customer to provide giveaways your first and immediate reaction is extremely important. If you react with any embarrassment, guilt, fear, hesitation or surprise you won't convey the right message to the customer. Never hesitate! If you're calm and confident and your body language suggests that, "Yes it's common for them to offer incentives," then you've appropriately established the parameters of your discussion with the customer.

Having set the scene you can proceed to discuss the reality of business with your customer. Some examples are:

"It's common for some suppliers to offer incentives. I guess they're not selling as much as they think they should be."

"Being able to give away so much reflects the true value of what they're offering."

"Do you really believe it's free? If it was really free they wouldn't be able to continue in business. They obviously include incentives in their cost of business. This indicates what the true cost of the product should be. It also provides you with an indication of the real quality of the product."

"If they were successfully selling their product do you think they'd be giving away money to entice people to do business with them?"

"What do you give away in your business to get people to deal with you?"

"What would you need to compromise on in your business if you gave away free products and services to obtain a new customer?"

Explain how your market reputation is too important for you to compromise the standards your organization has set for itself. And that if you don't charge a fair price you're unable to provide the service you promise.

After all, your customers appreciate your quality long after a "freebie" has been forgotten.

OK, if I have to...

You'll be surprised how many times, despite a correctly executed sale and the kind of discussions we've already described and recommended, the customer doesn't continue to pursue the request for a discount.

If your customer is still intent on asking you for a free giveaway and you have some scope to give something to them because you built an additional margin into your proposed pricing, you might provide a nominal discount as a show of good faith. This should only be done after you've confirmed with the customer that they're in a position to place the order with you. Such discounts should be between two and five percent on the initial price proposed. Never offer more than five percent discount in this situation.

Sales incentive giveaways are best used to close business quicker than the customer had intended.

2.8

Signed, sealed and ordered

This is the final and often the quickest step of a successful sale, proof-positive that all your hard work was worth the effort.

Once you have a green light to proceed from your customer don't waste time in getting the signature. Don't leave anything to chance as, unfortunately, a verbal order is not the same as a signed written order.

If you have multiple sales forms and documents in your industry and they all need to be completed, ensure that you have them all when you meet with the customer. Don't waste time by having to revisit the customer to amend paperwork. Ensure that any special conditions negotiated, or delivery / implementation instructions are all in writing. Don't leave any details to personal interpretation. Future queries or disputes will cost you valuable selling time. Document all points that have been agreed to.

If an error is made, or an alteration is required on the paperwork, ensure that the customer acknowledges the amendment by "initialing" next to the alteration. Again, this level of clarity will prevent frustrating distractions and loss of selling time.

Explain the delivery procedure, timeframes or execution of your solution to your new customer. Don't over promise and be sure to work within the operating constraints of your company. Make it clear to the customer when you'll next contact them and then move on to your next sale. Leave the customer with a clear understanding about when and how delivery and installation of the product or service will occur. This will save you time and reduce the need for further questions.

Be sure to thank the customer for their business and don't appear as if you take this for granted.

Why did they pick you?

If possible, find out why they selected you and your product over your competitors.

You may have won the business for reasons that you're not aware of. This question may also provide you with valuable information about what your competitors are saying and how they are selling. If you have the chance to look at competitors' quotes, or better still, you're able to grab a copy, it will tell you what competitive advantages they are promoting. This will help you in future sales.

Now that your potential customer has become an actual customer they represent many more future sales. Move on by looking for your next sale and don't waste time planning how you'll spend any commission you may be about to receive. Remind yourself that it's a sales department and that you're only as good as your last sale.

Follow-up

Once the product's installation or solution has been executed you should follow up with your customer and confirm that everything is to their satisfaction. Following this, leave the customer alone and let them get back to their work as it's likely they would have had their fill of sales people for the time being!

Based on what the future potential is to sell additional or repeat products to this customer, plan the timing of your next visit accordingly. In the same manner that you're calling on your competitors' customers, your competitors are calling on your customers. It's not the customer's job to contact you when they next have a need for one of your products. It's your job to anticipate that need and be there at the right time.

In business, circumstances change all the time and you may not need to wait an extended period of time before you have a chance to sell an additional product or solution to your customer. Any number of scenarios could occur which could lead to you securing more sales orders from your new customer.

For example:

- Additional requirements in other departments.
- Additional requirements in other locations.
- Expansion of business causing greater demand.
- Customer may acquire other businesses and have increased need for your product or solutions.

As the customer's staff come and go it is useful to make yourself known to the new person in the job. Similarly, getting to know more than one contact person can help to keep you top of mind if your primary contact leaves the organization.

Following a sale it's all too easy to take your success for granted and become complacent, or even lazy in your approach. Don't become a victim of your success. Remember what you've done to bring you this success and aim to not only repeat it, but build upon it.

Continue to do the things that have brought you success; most likely it will be diligence and repetitive, hard work.

2.9

Sorry about your loss

Being on the wrong side of success is rarely a good feeling. If you learn of your customer's decision to select a competitor's product over yours there are still a few things you can do.

First, it's not over until it's over! Clarify that the order has already been placed with your competitor. If the decision has been made, but not executed it's not yet lost.

In many instances it's difficult to change a customer's mind, but it can be done. Find out why they're considering your competitor. Misunderstandings and miscommunication can occur during the sales process and you want to eliminate these factors as reasons for losing the order.

If it's truly over, always remain calm, polite, professional and sincere. Be graceful in defeat and don't let your disappointment get the better of you. You have nothing to gain in being unprofessional.

You may choose to send them a letter or an email and thank them for their time, wishing them luck with their chosen supplier. This reaffirms you as a true professional and it may keep the door open for you in the future.

Find out why you lost the order
This is an extremely valuable exercise. Ask the customer for feedback if they don't go with your product. You might think that you know why

they decided to go to a particular supplier when you learn who they selected, but don't assume this. Listen to the customer's feedback. You'll gain valuable knowledge about what your competitors are selling and saying in the marketplace. This will help you plan your future presentations and negotiations.

Also ask for feedback about your presentation and your solution. What concerns did they have about selecting your solution? This knowledge is also valuable and can turn an unpleasant experience into a learning opportunity – perhaps even a profitable one in the future.

Once the sale is lost and you've learnt as much as you can from the situation, stop wasting time and move on to the next one. Retain a positive outlook and devote your energy to the next customer.

The neglected step of the sale

After losing a deal, many sales people understandably choose to ignore that customer for an extended period of time. A follow-up visit or phone call in six months is often worthwhile to see if the customer was happy with their new product. You may learn about product short-falls, or after sale service which has not been as promised. In extreme cases, disappointed or even angry customers may wish to be used as a negative referral site. You might learn about aspects of your competitor's solution which allows you to promote alternative aspects of your own solution to your advantage.

If the customer has had a bad experience, by contacting them and staying in touch, you may be considered for their other requirements. Without a follow-up call you may have incorrectly assumed that there was no opportunity with that customer for quite some time.

Having such an open-minded approach is difficult to adopt, especially when it involves deals that you've lost. However, by persevering with this approach you'll continue to edge out your competition as you work your way towards dominating your sales territory in your market.

Quick recap: The 7 steps of a sale

Every sale, particularly in business-to-business, has a natural series of steps. By understanding the 7 steps of a sale, you can act to position your product as the most preferred option in the customer's mind.

Following these steps not only helps you maximize the chance of securing the order, it also helps you sell at higher price points, obtaining higher gross profit.

Your pipeline

Selling is about numbers. The more you put into your sales pipeline, the more you'll reap at the end. Better results are obtained when quality numbers are pursued.

Chase potential customers who offer the greatest chance of success. Your time is limited!

Potential customers aren't going to call you. Don't waste time or leave anything to chance. Seek out new business and go for opportunity, even if it's disguised as disciplined and repetitive work.

Your first meeting

The first appointment is a really important stage in a potential sale that lets you set the tone and places you and your product at the "top of the pile" in the customer's mind.

The longer a sale takes to conclude, the more disillusioned the customer may become with "sales people" and their constant follow-up and interruptions. It's your job to ask focused questions to make the customer think seriously about their needs. And you need to do all of this in as short a time as possible.

If you can separate yourself as the preferred option early, it tends to make the rest of the process easier and less competitive.

Your show

Impressing your customer with a customized show, crafted specifically to address their needs, is a fantastic way to elevate the appeal of your product.

Go to whatever extent is practical in order to engage the customer's emotions. Impress them by introducing a level of enjoyment that compels them to deal with you. Things become easier when a customer decides they want to deal with you.

Your written proposal

By providing a proposal, showing how you can assist your customer, you're demonstrating your attention to detail and this conveys security – something that most customers are indirectly looking for.

Conducting another meeting, specifically to discuss your proposal and your product, provides a valuable selling opportunity.

Your negotiating skills

You'll lose few sales when dealing with reasonable customers if you take the time to openly discuss any differences that may exist between what you want and what they want or understand.

Negotiating should be seen as another discussion, albeit with the sales person having the benefit of experience. When it comes to a detailed discussion about their product, a sales person has the advantage of doing this every day, so an outcome in their favor is more likely.

Your learning curve

Understanding why you lost a sale is a more important – and more profitable – use of your time than most sales people appreciate.

Knowing what *not* to do next time will help turn your next lost order into a successful sales order.

Stories from the front line

Elly's new job

Elly was a bright girl, captain of the cheer-leading team and with the highest grade point average in her school. She was one of those people who "had it all." She was confident, motivated, attractive and capable of strategic thinking, despite her youth.

Elly was also blessed with highly effective interpersonal skills and could communicate with whomever she met. After college she was keen to discover the world, traveling and working her way around Europe and the Middle East for 18 months before returning home, eager to start a career. Her options and opportunities seemed endless.

From her studies, Elly knew the quickest way to the top of any organization was through the sales department. She understood on a fundamental level that business and commerce basically came down to selling a product or a service. Through her reading and research she believed that Company Presidents and Executives with sales, rather than an accountancy background, were more successful. She wanted to learn the skills of selling and she was thrilled when her application at the town's third-largest office equipment supplier was successful.

While friends and family were a little bewildered by her choice and thought she had undersold herself, Elly was ecstatic. She had a friend who worked for a similar company upstate and she knew that he was making excellent money. Elly was confident she was on the right path by starting a job in direct sales where she was paid based on the value that she brought to the company. She despised the thought of static remuneration based on length of service rather than actual contribution.

Mr. Wildon was the family's next door neighbor. He was an elderly gentleman, exceptionally polite and quiet. While growing up, Elly had spent many hours listening to some of his career stories about selling encyclopedia door-to-door. While he had long since retired, he worked at the same job for many decades and managed to put all five of his children through college. He had wisdom and a worldly outlook which Elly loved and aspired to replicate. Mr. Wildon was the one person who was most positive about Elly's news of her new job.

Before starting, Elly explained her new job to her family. She was really enthusiastic, but her family were more concerned about how hard it would be to cold-call and find sales leads. Elly brushed aside their comments. She had heard the term "call reluctance" from the sales manager during her interview. She had known that her new career in direct sales involved physically calling in on customers and telephoning potential customers to make appointments to see them. This aspect of her new role was not a concern to her because she clearly understood that sales is a numbers game. The more potential customer calls she made, the more money she would make, as the role was 100% commission on sales achieved. In fact, it was this aspect of the job that attracted her the most. Call reluctance was not an issue for her!

Enthusiasm

Elly started her new job with what can only be described as "gusto". One hundred and ten percent enthusiasm, diligence and dedication. She read all the brochures and sales guides, went out into the field with experienced sales people. She took it upon herself to speak to the company's technicians to learn as much as she could about their products. She also read all of the independent product reviews.

Elly wasn't waiting for the world to come to her; she made it her business to educate herself. There would be no excuses for lack of knowledge. Having read most of the available literature she spent time learning how to operate the machines. She played with all the functions and capabilities on both the software and hardware products the company offered. She made plans and created timetables to achieve certain milestones. She telephoned current customers to introduce herself as the new point of contact and to make sure that they were happy. If she did find a customer issue she pursued the service manager before getting back to the customer with answers.

Elly also studied the company's computerized service records to understand the information available. She spent many hours on the internet and learned all she could about her competitors. Next she made it her business to understand all the aspects and components of the sales database. She wasn't impressed with the proposal and quotation templates the company provided, so, with a sense of urgency she set about improving them.

Call reluctance

Ten days into her selling career, Elly had what's called a "light bulb moment." She took a long hard look at herself and realized with sudden clarity what "call reluctance" actually meant.

Every time Elly went to telephone a potential customer, she suddenly found another more important task instead. If she was honest with herself she knew that she had made every possible excuse not to call. In some strange way it was confronting to call a complete stranger and it made her nervous even thinking about it.

Curiously, Elly's sales manager didn't spot Elly's call reluctance because he was blinded by her work ethic and enthusiasm. In her heart Elly knew it was there and she knew it was real. She worried about rejection. What if they were rude? What if no one would meet her? Surely they would call her if they needed anything, so why did she need to call them?

When visiting existing customers in the field she had thought of cold-calling by walking into a company unannounced. She had even tried it twice. The first time she backed out when she saw others in the reception area. They looked like customers, not other sales people, and it didn't seem right to go in with an audience watching. The second time she almost managed to open the door, but as she looked through the glass door her heart began to beat faster and faster and her mouth just dried up. She didn't know what to say and the receptionist looked so busy taking phone calls she thought it best not to disturb her.

Elly never expected sales to feel like this. Now she truly knew what call reluctance was and it was personal, lonely and surprisingly confronting. Elly knew she could drive around in traffic for an hour and a half before it was an acceptable time to return to the office. Which is exactly what she did. She was relieved that it was Friday so she could take two days to hide and think about things. Not happy with herself she spent the night in, thinking about what job she should do and how best to solve this awful feeling she had. Elly was always honest with herself; she wasn't one to pretend, but the thought of failing bothered her, really bothered her.

Wildon's wisdom

On Saturday morning she called Mr. Wildon who agreed to have lunch with her. She felt that he would be a great sounding board for her concerns. Even if he could offer no real answers he was sure to be able to offer comfort by telling her that sales was not for everyone and she would feel better about handing in her resignation on Monday.

Elly relayed her fears to Mr. Wildon with an honesty that most people cannot muster. Mr. Wildon listened to Elly's story, especially when she displayed genuine surprise that she had any fear at all, given how popular, confident and successful she had always been. With an entire career devoted to direct sales, Mr. Wildon understood her concerns.

Mr. Wildon told her that cold calling and generating sales, like any skill, was something that had to be done again and again in order to perfect. He explained that if and when people didn't want her products it wasn't actually about Elly the person, but rather Elly's job. He told her to expect judgment and even bald-faced lies simply because of her job title. No matter what was thrown at her, Mr. Wildon believed that the trick was always to be polite, genuine, respectful and courteous to whomever she met.

He recalled how many times in his career on a return call (when someone had been abrupt and rude the first time) they were completely different the second time around. While he remembered how he had been treated the first time, often the customer had no such recollection and was perfectly polite.

Mr. Wildon also explained how cold-calling is about timing; as we don't have a crystal ball we don't know the "right" time to call. Consequently, we need to repeatedly call until we strike upon the right time, when the potential customer is interested. From years of practice, Mr. Wildon had learnt that persistence really does payoff. He wrote an address on a piece of paper and suggested that she go to level 5 of the particular building as there were some ladies and gentlemen there who would help her with her fears. He wished her all the best and hoped to hear from her soon.

It's about perspective

Monday morning arrived sooner than expected and, while Elly was still apprehensive, she headed out into the field under the guise of cold-calling and generating business. Her first stop was the building that Mr. Wildon had said to attend. Elly assumed that the building must have some of Mr. Wildon's associates working on reception. She was sure that they would be friendly and she would begin to build her confidence cold-calling.

Elly parked her car and walked the remaining block or so looking for the right address. She passed a bus stop with a poster advertising a charity that was raising money for victims somewhere in the Far East where an earthquake had destroyed people's homes. She passed the same poster several times while looking for the office block, but found herself standing outside the County Hospital. Finally it dawned on her that there must be administration offices inside the hospital.

When the lift opened on the fifth floor, Elly found herself standing in the middle of a busy hospital ward. Nurses, doctors, patients and visitors seemed to be moving at break-neck speed all around her. Elly felt overwhelmed by the sight of sick children without hair, distressed parents sitting anxiously by babies who struggled for breath.

Elly was shocked by what she saw as she walked around the ward. So much so that she decided to spend the afternoon walking along a beach, trying to make sense of the issues these children had, compared to the issues she thought she had.

The next morning Elly went back to work expecting to be questioned about her absence. To her surprise no one had noticed she'd been gone, nor did they question her whereabouts. Everyone assumed she was in the field doing her job.

After some hours of contemplation, Elly came to a startling realization. Making a telephone call, walking into a reception area, worrying about what someone may think of her suddenly didn't seem like a big deal. Elly set about cold-calling and telemarketing with a changed view of the world. She had always had a positive and mature attitude, but an unscheduled trip to the hospital had literally opened her eyes and changed her perspective on everything.

Elly didn't hand in her resignation as planned. By attacking, not ignoring, her fear of cold-calling, Elly was able to get out of her comfort zone. This helped her improve, grow and become a more qualified and accomplished person. Like most sales people, Elly had her ups and downs but she never looked backed.

Part 3: What's your sales story?

Setting yourself apart from your competition will happen the more you appreciate the need to follow the steps of the sale. This will be further enhanced once you develop your sales stories and selling arguments.

Knowing what you're selling and having clarity about why your customer should select you and your solution will see you dominate your marketplace. You'll regularly beat your less-educated competitors.

In this part:
What are we *really* selling?
Competitive advantage
Emotional reality
Help them fall

3.1

What are we really selling?

We deliberately avoid complex sales theories and over-analysis in this book. Instead, we believe it's more important for sales people to question and appreciate what they're actually doing in business-to-business selling.

"So, what are we *really* selling?"

The obvious answer is whatever product or solution it is that you sell. While superficially that's true, it's not the best answer.

A more thoughtful answer could be:

"We're actually selling ourselves, as well as solutions to customer needs."

This response is also correct. In fact, it's probably fair to assume that most of your competitors think like this. So let's go one step further.

Ask yourself, "What *should* we be selling?"

As previously discussed, there are three distinct topics you'll inevitably cover in any given sale. These are:

- Product / service – the actual item being sold.
- Service support – support after the sale transaction.
- Payment method.

To promote a total solution you should be discussing the customer's requirements in *each* of these three areas. Consequently, we're selling a product or service, a post- sale support service and a payment method.

Selling a 'post-sale service' or, if applicable, 'a payment method' is not selling a physical thing. It's considered to be an intangible (something that can't be physically seen and touched).

This can then raise another question, "Are we selling a tangible or an intangible product?"

Typically, you'll be selling both tangible and intangible products. In most situations we sell the tangible product and the intangible of the after sales service or payment method.

When sales people sell intangibles like services they don't have the comfort of pointing to a physical product. They can't talk about the physical functions and capabilities of the product.

Consequently, there is a natural tendency for sales people who are selling intangible products such as services to talk about "what the agreement provides" or "what the service does" for the customer, how it benefits them. They find it easier to demonstrate what the service *provides*, as opposed to simply talking about what the service actually *is*.

The key to selling correctly is to always talk in terms of what your product or solution *does* for your customer, i.e. how it benefits them. This is the key to what should be "sold" to the customer by all sales people who sell tangible and intangible products.

Benefits not features

We should be presenting and discussing the benefits of our products. We must always think in terms of what advantage the customer will gain from a given feature or aspect of our product. We must know what benefit a given feature offers a customer. This applies to both our tangible products and the intangible components of our solution (service and payment terms).

By way of example, let's assume the product we are selling is a glass-faced touch screen smart phone used for business purposes. The customer in our example is an insurance company claims assessor who travels from place to place inspecting damaged motor vehicles that are subject to a claim.

Few customers would desire a glass-faced phone that may be easily broken if dropped, or one that needs to always be protected from the heat of direct sunlight and kept away from all things wet. So in this example, consider what's actually being sold to the customer.

There's little appeal and sense about the actual product, the tangible product, as very few people would desire an easily broken glass-faced telephone. However a feature of the device is the ability to write and receive emails. This translates into the advantage that the customer can be anywhere and is not bound to be in the office to check their email.

The reason this customer wants to purchase the phone is because it saves him time by not having to go back to the office to collect his next inspection job. This enables him to complete his daily tasks quicker and by completing his work quicker he is at the beach at 4.30pm each afternoon. Having a cell phone provides this customer the *benefit* of completing his work early enough each day to go for his daily swim. This is the *real* benefit this customer derives from buying this product.

Ultimately, it's the intangible benefit that excites and holds the most weight in the sales process. So we should always be selling the intangible benefits our product provides.

We're selling intangibles

While our products have many features and attributes, in reality few potential customers will be enthused by these features. However, when we focus on the advantages or benefits these features provide, our potential customers become enthusiastic.

Take a moment and write a list of your main product features, including:

- Product – what does your product do, what are the capabilities and functions?
- Service support – what are the after-sales services and capabilities?
- Payment method – what is the structure of the payment method?

Next to each feature write the advantage and/or benefit that the feature could provide to a potential customer. You'll very quickly note that a given feature may have different benefits to customers.

Consider our basic smart phone as an example.

Features (to name only a few):

- Small and compact.
- Large electronic keypad.
- Built-in speaker and microphone.
- Password-protected pin code.
- Quick start camera.
- High resolution camera.
- Keeps history of calls received and made.

Benefit or advantage of feature:

Consider the second feature mentioned above, the large electronic keypad. This can provide the benefits of say,

- The large numbers make it easier to read.
- Buttons and keypad numbers may not wear out like manual buttons.
- Keypad can be seen at night.

If you think – and talk – in terms of advantages and benefits when you make your sales presentations, you're more likely to engender enthusiasm in the customer.

Telling someone your product has a large electronic keypad may not mean much to them, but discussing the fact that when they are out at night for a walk they can easily see the numbers to dial home and check on the kids will carry more weight and mean something to the customer and may have value to them.

Explaining how the keypad accommodates adult-sized fingers so that you can easily dial telephone numbers without hitting the wrong number may be something the customer can relate to if they've experienced the frustrations and cost of dialing incorrect numbers.

We're selling advantages and benefits

Because we're selling our product's intangible advantages and benefits, this further validates the need to sell by asking questions.

You'll never get an opportunity to discuss every advantage and benefit that your product provides. The key is to ask questions that establish what's of greatest importance to the customer. Being the sales person you know the benefits and advantages that your product or solution can provide. So you need to ask questions that uncover the customer's needs or wants – the needs and wants that your product can solve.

Continuing with our simple example, if we establish the customer has issues with the size of their fingers compared to the keypad button size on their existing cell phone then we know it's valid to discuss this benefit.

If we then tell the story of the customer going for a walk and needing to see the numbers at night it's not solving a problem for them, there's no appeal for this customer. We need to tell them about the reason for the size of the buttons, i.e. to avoid dialing the wrong number and incurring a cost for the incorrect call. This will impress the customer and they will start to value the product on offer – because it solves their problem.

We ask questions to establish which benefits are most relevant to the customer. We only sell the applicable benefits that this customer values as it solves a problem for them. In sales, we're always trying to solve customer problems.

We're selling solutions to problems

This perspective will help you to present your sales story in a way that's more in tune with each customer's needs and concerns.

The more benefits you can present which are valuable and important to a customer, the more they will see your solution as the most appropriate option for them. The more problems and potential problems for which you have a solution, the more the customer will value and desire what you're offering.

It follows that different benefits are attractive to different prospects.

We're selling what our customer wants

In our earlier example, one customer likes the product as they can see the size of the numbers on the keypad, despite their aging eyesight. Another is drawn to the product as they're easily able to press the keypad numbers without touching an incorrect digit, saving them time and money calling wrong numbers. A third customer values the product as they can see the keypad numbers easily and quickly when they are out at night.

We've actually sold three different solutions. While it's all based on the same physical product and the same product feature, we've sold a customized solution that meets a specific need for each customer.

Again, keep asking questions

By asking questions, we know what to "sell" to the particular customer.

We simply tailor our discussions and sales stories around what it is that the customer can relate to. Because we ask many questions and know what benefits our solution can provide we know to concentrate discussions on those benefits that have relevance and importance to the particular customer. We can't risk talking about generic benefits that we "think" may be appropriate. We need to ensure that the benefit is appropriate and valued by the particular customer we are selling to.

For example, by advising that the keypad is large enough for adult fingers you may offend a potential customer as they could interpret the comment to mean that they have "fat fingers." Not only is there no value in highlighting this benefit, but it could have a detrimental effect on obtaining the sale. So you structure your sales stories based on what each particular customer wants.

Too much to talk about

We seek to sell a total solution about the product, after-sale service and payment method. Within each category we'll have numerous features and consequently multiple advantages and benefits. This means the scope for sales discussion is enormous, regardless of the simplicity of the product. So it should be easy for you to talk in terms of benefits to the customer.

The unspoken motivator

Different customers will see merit in different parts of our solution, but most customers share some fundamental concerns that help to motivate and influence their purchasing decisions.

Customers who are buying on behalf of a business generally don't want their decision to appear a foolish one, especially to their work colleagues. They don't want the product or service to fail, or the after-sale service to be lacking.

The decision maker responsible for choosing the product is likely to have an underlying concern about its reliability if you're a new supplier. But they're unlikely to voice these concerns.

In addition to solving the customer's specific problems, it's also helpful to structure your discussions and presentation around conveying a peace of mind or the security that your solution offers, compared to your competitors.

We're selling the security of the safest option

When we build a case as the best solution provider for the customer, we're dealing in emotions and perceptions, not just facts and logic. Don't underestimate the power emotions play in a business decision. Always position your product as the safest available option for the customer to select.

This will be valued, despite the fact that the customer is unlikely to identify this to you. By positioning your solution as the most "fail-safe" it'll always add to your chances of success.

3.2

Competitive advantage

Competition is a given. Extreme competition is common in most markets. You have to accept this and move on.

The only way to beat your competitors is to set yourself apart from them. The objective is to be somehow different and to be viewed as being different by the customer.

Understand how they see you

While you may see yourself as distinct from those you compete against, it's important to appreciate where the customer, who hasn't met you or your company, is starting from when you first attempt to meet with them.

To better appreciate your customer's view of your industry, look in your local business directory for a product type you have little knowledge of. For example, roof restoration, window double-glazing, or insect pest control suppliers.

You'll see advertisements and listings for several suppliers, whichever category you select. On face value most suppliers will appear to be the same to you. It's valid to suggest that you are indifferent in your preference because they appear that way. The reality may be that out of ten suppliers you look at:

- Some will be very reliable and have good quality offerings.
- Some will have only acceptable quality to offer.
- Some will take your business for granted and be difficult to deal with.
- Some will provide poor quality products and service.
- One may not be totally honest, even unethical.

Your initial perception and the reality of the supplier options are often greatly different.

This lack of appreciation of the reality is also the starting point for your customers. They see you in the same way as you see the "double glazing" list of suppliers. The customer may not have knowledge of your industry, so the starting point of their decision-making process is that all suppliers look the same.

Remind yourself of this as you craft your sales stories around the competitive advantages you offer.

Your competitive advantage

Do you know your competitive advantage in your marketplace?

While competitive advantage varies from supplier to supplier and from market to market, you need to be very clear about what your product offers that your competitors do not.

Ask yourself:

- Why should your customers buy products from you?
- How is your product different?
- Why is your product the best and most appropriate option?
- Why is your product the safest, most secure, lowest risk option available?

The reasons why your product, service support system and payment methods are superior may be many and varied.

Your answers to the above questions will form the basis of your sales story.

Who tells a better sales story wins

Regardless of how well your sales story is crafted, including your competitive advantages, there is always an opposite story. When presented in context this story may also seem plausible, if not more beneficial.

For example, a ten-person insurance broking company with one office has a need for a printer / scanning machine. They also need a new computer network support supplier.

One supplier sells printers and scanning products and they service printer machines. They also have a computer network support service department.

A second supplier sells printers and scanning products, along with the service these machines may require, but they don't supply computer network support services.

The sales people for each supplier base part of their sales story on the following points:

Supplier 1 provides printer / scanners and computer network support services.

- Offers an integrated solution.
- Customer only needs to make one telephone call for any issue with a printer or the computer network.
- Customer will never have an issue with the computer network people blaming the printer for a fault and vice versa for any printer malfunction, as they are responsible for both.
- Supplier has a more intimate knowledge of the workings of the entire system, providing a greater ability to prevent problems or fix issues quickly.
- Customer only has one monthly invoice to process.

Supplier 2 provides printers / scanners only.

- Supplier is a specialist. It makes better business sense to deal with "a master craftsman" as opposed to a "jack of all trades."
- Using one supplier implies greater risk if the supplier doesn't perform.
- Given the nature of support roles (printer / scanner technician and Computer Network Engineer), different engineers are needed, even if they're employed by the same company, because they are two different skill sets.
- Supplier has a more detailed discussion about the printer / scanner print quality, scan quality and machine functionality and how it will benefit the customer.
- Supplier also has detailed discussion about how service fault response times would be achieved and the technology in the printer / scanner which enhances reliability and print quality to minimize after-sale service requirements.
- Separate, specific invoices prevent confusion and clarity for allocation of costs and allow for easier auditing.

Which sales story is better? Which sales story is more correct? Which scenario would you favor? Which one would the potential customer favor? Who has the greater competitive advantage?

Both sales arguments are equally plausible. The sales person who will win the sale will be the one who asked the customer questions and ascertained what was important to them; then they delivered those aspects of their sales story in the best way to appeal to the customer.

You, the sales person are the competitive advantage

Take this to the next stage and envisage a scenario where two solutions are in every way identical. Product, service support systems and payment methods are exactly the same.

As we know, the only difference between sales offerings to the customer in this scenario would be the sales person. Two identical solutions could be presented in totally different ways as a result of a sales person's skill and their approach to the sale.

How you go about your role is your ultimate competitive advantage.

As products and services develop it is usual that no competitive advantage based on functionality or operational benefits will exist for long as suppliers copy one another. Therefore the importance of developing your own style and approach to the sale cannot be overstated.

Your performance during the steps of the sale is the major component in obtaining an order. Your attention to detail, responsiveness and clear communication style will be your major competitive advantage. Critically important, it's an advantage which no competitor can ever replicate. It's a unique competitive advantage.

You should never underestimate the impact you have on a customer's purchasing decision. They first choose someone they are happy to deal with, followed by an assessment of company reputation and only then do they consider if the product actually meets their needs.

If sales people really had no influence on purchasing decisions then all products would be exclusively sold over the internet by each and every manufacturer.

Avoid generic sales claims

As you develop and improve your competitive advantage sales stories you'll make various sale claims to your customers. With experience, you could deliver your version of the following statements with confidence and conviction:

> "...our product is superior quality within our marketplace."
> "...we have such a large market share because our product is the best value for money in the market today."

"....I'm lucky because we have the best quality option available at present."

"...I know that every sales person will sit here and tell you they have the best product and after-sale support program, but we actually do what we say."

"....we're proud to give you the best quality at the lowest possible price due to our buying power."

What the potential customer heard may not be what you thought you said, or meant to say. The potential customer may be thinking:

"Well everyone says that."

"'These sales people are all the same."

"What else would you say if you're expecting me to buy something from you?"

An experienced sales person should not make generic claims. They add no value. They make you look and sound like your competitors which is the opposite of your objective! Generic statements should not be used by the professional sales person.

Be more business-like
Take a slightly different thought process into your sales presentations.

Be more business-like with your sales stories. For example, if asked about your response time to post-sale service issues, start by acknowledging to your potential customer that:

"All sales people will tell you the same thing, or tell you what you want to hear. Most of them will be long gone by the time your product is two years old. Let me explain the system we have in place so you know you'll have service long after any sales claims that we make."

Continue to explain what your past and current service response times are, how you track and monitor them and your method of working.

Explain the systems and training that are in place to ensure your company's after-sale service is acceptable to your customers.

These in-depth discussions grab the interest of your customer.

Taking this approach elevates the quality of discussions and most of your competitor sales people will fail to cope with this.

Avoid the big claim

Ask yourself if you can 100% guarantee any claim that you make. For example, can you 100 % guarantee that:

- You have the best quality product available?
- Your product will never fail?
- Your support systems are faultless?

If you can see into the future with a crystal ball you may be able to guarantee it. Failing that, it's a sales claim with no real value. If you can't guarantee something in your sales story then don't make the claim.

Having more detailed discussions with your customer about why your product could be considered superior quality and outlining the practical justifications and examples, is far more powerful than claiming that it's the "best." Everyone claims they have the best product, service or value. Always explain the reason behind your competitive advantage and don't make general sales claims.

Customers will listen to these discussions. Once you can present and sell from this viewpoint you'll soon be dominating your sales territory.

Subtle competitive advantages

Sometimes competitive advantages aren't necessarily sales stories. They can be other factors, like the way you conduct yourself.

As subtle as it may appear, shaking hands with your customer as you greet them can be a slight advantage. Always make eye contact with your customer when you shake hands. Sales people are often preoccupied and too busy for these things, instead pulling their chair out, picking up their briefcase, or thinking about their next sentence. Deliberately take a few seconds and eyeball your customer when you shake hands, as most people don't consistently do this.

Listening can also be an advantage to you. As we may hear the same request from different customers five times a day, it becomes difficult to listen politely without interrupting so we can speed things up. The customer only gets the chance to talk about their requirements once every so often so it's important to them. We should listen and let them have their say.

Conducting two sales calls as opposed to one can be a competitive advantage. Having a repeat meeting with a customer's colleague or superior may translate into a competitive advantage. It might help secure the sale because you were prepared to repeat a step of the sale.

Product shortfalls

In addition to knowing your product in order to build your competitive advantage sales stories, you should also try to establish the reason behind perceived shortfalls of your product. These are the functions that competitors' products offer, but your product may not be equipped with.

Armed with an understanding as to why a product has been designed in a certain way, "shortfalls" often turn out to be deliberate and can actually unveil advantages.

Blurring the lines

Most likely, other suppliers within your geographical area will sell the same or similar products and services as you. It therefore makes sense to more heavily promote competitive advantages that relate to you as a supplier, as opposed to selling your potential customer on your product or brand, only to have them buy it from another supplier.

If your sales stories blur the lines between product benefits and service support benefits it sends a very powerful message.

For example, your customer may ask you about the particular characteristics of your product. If you explain the product characteristics and also discuss how your after-sale support relates to this product feature, e.g. how the after-sale service ensures that the product continually performs optimally, you're then blurring the lines between product and after-sale support.

If your customer is asking you about the payment terms and in answering this you can relate how certain attributes of the product complement the payment arrangements due to the product's lifespan, you're selling in a manner that few other sales people will attempt. Obviously this is a product-dependent approach, but mixing of messages will be possible for most products if you take the time to consider different scenarios.

By selling in this manner you shouldn't answer a product question with an answer that's limited to the product. And you don't answer a service question with an answer that's limited to the service.

When appropriate, you should always mix the selling messages when they relate to the topic you're discussing. This way you're promoting your appropriateness as a supplier.

Work as a team
Team selling can be a great competitive advantage. When more than one person tells the same story it sends a strong message to your customer. A Sales Manager or Sales Supervisor can contact a sales person's customer and seek information that the sales person was unable to establish. At times, the customer's perception that they are dealing with someone of greater authority yields more candid responses about their situation.

Team selling has its shortfalls and risks. Two different selling styles could unsettle the customer. Both the sales person and Sales Manager must think alike with respect to obtaining a profitable sale.

Team selling is always worth consideration, but can be expensive having two people doing one person's job.

3.3

Emotional reality

Our behavior is often driven by emotion.

As we work through the steps of the sale we need to be continually aware of our emotions and how they don't necessarily reflect reality.

You need to keep your emotions in check as you work towards your goal. Don't confuse "passion" with being emotional. You need to be passionate about your work, but being emotional rarely yields the required result. It's easy for sales people to become emotional and to be distracted by things. This can happen when:

- Customers lie to you.
- Customers don't take your telephone call.
- Customers don't return your messages or emails.
- You experience tough competition in the marketplace.
- Competitors are dishonest when obtaining new customers.

All of the above distractions are to be expected, but they don't warrant further discussion or frustration. These things will regularly occur. Don't waste your time by getting angry about issues that are part of normal business-to-business direct sales. Set your emotions and frustrations aside and move on.

Their perception is your reality

Selling isn't entirely about solving problems. When dealing with customers, always remind yourself that it's the customer's perception of the situation that matters. It's not about your perception.

Our approach to sales is essentially one based on fear. We indirectly promote the idea that if the customer doesn't select our solution they will have greater risk. By asking so many questions and being thorough in our sales arguments we educate the customer about our industry. We present our sales story using supporting documentation and other facts. Our approach is based on logic and detail.

We choose this approach as it's the best way to maximize appeal to the infinite variety of customers we encounter. It's also the best way to differentiate ourselves from our competitors.

But beware. All the logic in the world can be quickly replaced by a customer's emotional decision. For this reason, you must ensure that your approach is indirectly tied to the emotion of greater risk if they don't select your solution.

Reality is of little consequence if the customer "thinks" a certain supplier has the best deal. A customer will always select the solution they perceive to be the most appropriate for them. The reality may be very different.

Consequently, in direct sales it's often the sales person who communicates the best sales story that wins. The one who wins the battle in the customer's mind. Not all business decisions are based on logic!

Customer justification

The value of this is that once you've made that breakthrough in your customer's mind and sold them on your solution, they'll easily justify it in their mind and within their organization. They do this to achieve what they feel is the best decision for them and their organization.

Consider some of the types of questions that we ask our customers; the questions which always yield the most valuable information:

"Do you feel that you've received value for money from your current supplier?"

"Do you think that your current product should have lasted longer?"

"Why didn't you automatically re-sign with your current supplier?"

The responses to these questions are based on how the customer *feels* about the situation. The factual reality is sometimes less relevant within the selling cycle.

Ironically, the responses we get to these more open questions about customers' feelings often reveal the most valuable information.

Emotional decisions

All your hard work has the potential to be quickly forgotten when a competitor is selling on emotions. A customer may rationalize their decision because:

"They gave us a free iPad."

"They had promotional pricing this month."

"They gave us a new model at old model prices."

Logic suggests that anything free is built into the final customer expenditure. Otherwise, the company couldn't afford to stay in business by giving away items for free, simply to get people to do business with them.

You need to be aware of this aspect of sales, as logic doesn't always win the sale. We don't suggest that you primarily sell in this manner because it's not a foolproof approach. For starters, most of your competitors may tend to operate in this way and we don't want to look like our competitors. It's more profitable to set ourselves apart from our competitors.

The lesson to be noted is that at times we do need to make the customer feel as if they've received a special deal.

Think of a friend or associate that recently purchased a new car. If you ask them about it or congratulate them, almost without exception they will automatically tell you how they got a good deal.

"We weren't going to go for it, but they gave us a good deal." These same people are the people who make decisions for businesses they represent. A company or business is comprised of people after all. Decisions aren't made by robots.

We all want to feel as if we received a fair deal. Be mindful of this when you structure your initial proposal – in case you do need to do something to make the customer feel that they're receiving a good deal.

3·4

Help them fall

Never specifically talk about competitors

While you should encourage your customers to talk about your competitors and the options they're considering, you should never use a competitor's name in your sales presentation. Never tell your customer what your competitor does and how they operate. It's OK to talk about "other suppliers" in general terms, but never specifically name a competitor or purport to be an expert about another company.

There is a clear distinction between using a competitor's name and talking in general terms about "others" in your industry. Most of your competing sales people won't hold back when it comes to sharing their opinion about their competitors and how they operate. A more professional approach will set you apart and portray you as someone less concerned about your competition.

As you talk in general terms, substitute competitor company names for words like "they," "other suppliers," "some people," etc. By speaking in this way, you'll raise doubt in the customer's mind about *all* of your competitors, not just the ones they may have highlighted.

Tripping your competitor sales people up and helping them to slip can dramatically increase your chances of securing the sales order. It's easy to out-maneuver your competition and effectively eliminate them from contention. With experience, the successful sales person anticipates typical customer objections and provides solutions before those objections are raised.

This can be taken one step further by promoting your solution in a way that also questions or casts doubt over your competitor's sales story.

Once you're aware of which suppliers the customer is considering, through experience you'll generally know what competitive advantage sales stories your competitors will be promoting.

Fortunately, many competitive sales people tell the same sales story over and over. They repeat the story that has brought them the most success and the one they're most comfortable with. This makes it easy for you to incorporate some comments into your sales story that refute, cast doubt over, or question your competitor.

In effect, you'll be beating your competitor before they get a chance to be heard.

Timing is everything

From the start of the selling cycle be selective about when you conduct each step of the sale relative to your competitors. For example, be keen to conduct your first appointment *before* competitors so you can set a high benchmark, but be slower to provide your proposal until *after* your competitors have provided theirs.

This way, the customer is able to give you an informed opinion about your proposed solution and how it compares.

The "sales trip"

Obviously there will be many ways that you can proactively create the impression that your competitor's sales story isn't genuine. The following generic examples illustrate the potential scope you may have to "trip" your competitor before they've had a chance to be heard by the customer.

Discussions designed to trip competitors are industry-specific by nature, but the example scenarios listed below will give you an idea. Each scenario could be a competitive advantage that your competitor typically promotes, or a sales approach they generally employ.

You can make these proactive comments in the course of telling the customer your sales story, indirectly critiquing your competitor's claims before they get a chance to sell to the customer.

Example 1: Competitor always has a lower-priced solution. Comments a sales person could make:

"We're not the cheapest option in our industry because we value quality and reliability above inferior solutions."
"There will always be someone cheaper, but our market reputation is too important to us to compromise on service and quality."
"The quality of our product doesn't enable us to supply at the lowest price point. At the end of the day, you get what you pay for."

Example 2: Competitor always engages in "give away" sales incentives when month-end is approaching to entice customers to order.

"The price points we propose will be realistic. Our competitors will offer all sorts of discounts and incentives at month's end. Our view is if they could have provided a lower price, why are they attempting to profiteer? We find that approach insincere. We assume you don't want us to build giveaways into our pricing proposal?"
"We're happy for you to proceed within your time-frame. We'll not be providing incentives to force you into a decision by the end of the month. We're not desperate for the sale this month, as others may be. We're happy to help you when you're ready to make a decision. Let me know when you're making a decision and we can talk more about the particulars."

"You watch, they'll all come back to you next week because it's month end and they'll be desperate to make their sales budget. If you consider making a decision sooner please let me know and I can come in and have another chat with you about the particulars and work within your time-frame. There's no rush from our viewpoint."

"We're very keen to help you, but, like yourself, I'm also very busy. So I won't be pestering you for a decision and calling you every two days as is common in our industry. Let me know when you're making a decision and I can bring you up to speed with any changes that may have occurred."

Example 3: Competitor generally includes a free offering towards the end of negotiations.

"Some competitors cost additional products and giveaways into their proposal then typically offer it as a "free" product or incentive after they provide their initial proposal. The need to offer these buying incentives is questionable, but if you do want a "free" incentive I can cost it into my proposal also. Would you like me to do so? We don't think it makes sense, but it's up to you."

Example 4: Competitor provides extensively written customer references in all sales presentations.

"If at any stage you'd like customer referrals please let me know, as we don't promote our solution by distracting customers with loads of written referrals. After all, there's no such thing as a bad reference, especially handpicked references. It's easy to get 15 or more letters. We prefer to explain our product's superior technology and our reliable back up service support systems. This means more to our potential customers."

Example 5: Competitor always involves their Sales Manager in their sales approach.

"You'll probably find that after you've received the proposal the Sales Manager will telephone you or will come out to meet you. They'll most likely be offering some sort of factory rebate or discount."

Example 6: Competitor promotes their competitive advantage as a small boutique local supplier.

"Our industry has become one where those with the greatest market share have economies of scale to provide the necessary customer support. For example, having the largest technical service engineer workforce affords us the luxury to take the time to properly train our field technical staff without compromising on our service response to customers. Smaller operations may not have this luxury of taking service engineers out of the field to train them properly, especially if this cuts their available field staff by 25%. Given the technology involved in our products, technical training is critically important."

Example 7: Competitor promotes their large market share.

"We don't have or seek to have the largest market share. We're quality-conscious so we only work with organizations that understand quality and reliability. These are people who appreciate that we do what we say we'll do, who don't want to get lost in our system and who prefer to speak to a local person if they ever have a query or problem."

Most of the discussions designed to trip your competitor can take place before your competitor has their chance in front of the customer.

Once you're aware of whom you are competing against, set them up for a fall – indirectly – as you tell your sales story.

When they do get to present their sales story, raising points and opinions which you've already cast doubt upon, their story actually adds credibility to *yours*. It's very satisfying to have your competitors indirectly validating your sales story!

Change your script

If we vary our sales story and sell our solutions in different ways to different customers, it will make it extremely difficult for our competitors to help *us* fall. We can easily vary our approach, given the vast array of sales stories we can present.

Work on your scripts from time to time to avoid being predictable.

Quick recap: What's your sales story?

The sales person who can tell a better story will always win the sales order. The more detailed the story – applicable to the particular customer's situation – the better the chance of success.

Know why you and your product are better than others available to the customer.

And always remember that a poor sales person with a superior product will always be beaten by a good sales person with an inferior product.

Your benefits (not features)

The key to selling correctly is to always talk in terms of what your product *does* for your customer, i.e. how it benefits them.

You should be discussing the benefits of your products and thinking in terms of what advantage the customer will gain from a given feature of your product.

We must know what benefit a given feature offers a customer. The key is to ask questions that establish what's of greatest importance to them.

Your safe option

Selling is all about identifying the problems you can solve for a customer, or identifying how you can improve a situation for them by demonstrating how your product is the best and safest option – for their particular circumstance.

By positioning your solution as the most "fail-safe" it will always add to your chances of success.

Your pre-emptive strike

You can make proactive comments in the course of telling the customer your sales story, indirectly critiquing your competitor's claims before they get a chance to sell to the customer.

Substitute competitors' company names for words like "they," or "other suppliers" and you'll raise doubt in the customer's mind about *all* of your competitors, not just the ones they may have highlighted.

Your emotions

Always pay attention to a customer's emotional view of the world. Keep your own emotions in check for optimal results and always be on your guard for the customer to be sidetracked by a competitor's emotional offer.

Use the customer's emotions to your advantage when circumstances permit and never forget that the customer's perception is reality to them.

Your competitive advantage

It makes sense to promote competitive advantages that relate to you as a supplier, as opposed to selling your potential customer on your product or brand, only to have them buy it from another supplier.

As a supplier solution you should be discussing your customer's requirements in each of three areas: (1) a product or service, (2) a post-sale support service and (3) a payment method.

Use your sales stories to blur the lines between product benefits and service support benefits as this sends a very powerful message.

If we vary our sales story and sell our solutions in different ways to different customers, it also makes it extremely difficult for your competitors to help you "fall".

Your unique advantage

You should never underestimate the impact you have on a customer's purchasing decision.

Your performance during the steps of the sale is the major component in obtaining an order. Your attention to detail, responsiveness and clear communication style will be your major competitive advantage. It's a unique advantage no competitor can ever replicate.

Part 4: But wait, there's more

As you work your way through each step of the sale and refine your approach you're certain to unearth a few more competitive advantages. These are advantages your competitors may not easily imitate as they're about the way *you* operate, not the way your *product* operates.

Remember that success in sales is all about you, how you think and how you approach your role.

In this part:
The "no doubt" attribute
It's a live performance
Moral compass
We're not alone
Two "golden rules"
That's not what I think I said
Future sales
Overwhelming, yet simple

4.1

The "no doubt" attribute

At each stage of the sales process you should present yourself as an expert, regardless of the actual length of service you've had in your industry. After all, you do this every day and your customer doesn't buy your products every day, nor are they working in your industry.

At times, customers use industry jargon they may have picked up from competitor sales people. Don't be misled or intimidated by this. Remember you're presenting to the customer because you're the expert. You know your solution better than they do.

At the very least, you can take some initial confidence from knowing that you do this every day – unlike the customer – before greater experience provides you with even more justification to sell with authority and confidence.

You need to believe at all times that you have the best available solution for the customer, regardless of their circumstance. The source of personal confidence is different for each of us. Some may gain it from their excellent product knowledge, some from their sales ability, or simply from years of experience. Wherever your sense of confidence comes from doesn't really matter. The key is simply to have it. Remember, people will not listen to you if they sense you don't truly believe what you're saying or selling.

Displaying a confident demeanor is comforting to the customer. Customers want to deal with someone who gives them a sense of security, someone who conveys that they know what they're talking about. Confidence without arrogance is unobtrusive and very comforting to the customer during the sales process. Lack of confidence will be noticed; it can even be incorrectly interpreted as dishonesty.

The seed of doubt

The seed of doubt is found at the back of a sales person's mind. Coincidentally, it's a similar shape to a peanut. It's the part of a sales person's mind responsible for fear and assumptions, especially assumptions about competitors.

Sometimes the seed of doubt is referred to as the "grass is greener" chip.

Ever present, the seed emits a constant message that your competitor may have a superior solution, or that they have a better value option for your customer. For most sales people it's not a dominating message. It can best be described as a constant background noise as they work their way through the selling cycle.

Where does the seed come from?

The seed develops in the sales person's mind in the third or fourth month of their sales career. It's absent for the first two months.

In those first two months sales people are blindly enthusiastic and can only see an abundance of opportunity everywhere they look. They lack product knowledge so they do more listening than talking with customers. They believe everything they are taught. They take to the sales field and do everything that they're employed to do, without question and without distraction. New sales people are blind to fear and the risk of losing a sales order as they've not yet experienced it. Most new sales people tend to sell more in their first two months than they do in their second two months.

Two kinds of events generally occur to create the seed of doubt:

- The sales person loses a potential sales order to a competitor for reasons they didn't think possible. It may have been lost to a lower-priced product or to a product with capabilities their option didn't possess.
- Upon receiving customer feedback the sales person discovers that their employer's products and service is not perfect and that they've made mistakes with some customers.

Whilst disappointing, these issues create fear; the fear of failing which dents the new sales person's confidence. Their pure enthusiasm and utter conviction is unfortunately tempered by real life experience.

It's important to deal with these negative experiences and put them into perspective.

Remind yourself that the world isn't perfect. There's no such thing as a perfect job, perfect employer, perfect product or perfect service support. In business, as in life, things can sometimes go wrong!

Customers can inadvertently have a bad experience. Just because your employer has room for improvement and some of their business systems may not be what you desire, it doesn't imply that your competitor is any better than your employer; your competitor will face similar challenges.

Understanding how to deal with a lost order is also very important when it comes to preventing the growth of your seed of doubt. If an order is lost this doesn't mean "doom and gloom" or failure. Take a step back from the deal and look at the way it played out. Acknowledge the things you did right. Assess the things you should've done better, or differently. Be fair to yourself by looking at the positives as well as the opportunity for improvement.

Removing the seed of doubt enables you to reach your full sales potential. Without exception, you must believe that you're the best sales person. You must operate with a mindset of certainty without compromise.

Consider the following as a kind of personal mantra:

"Give me the worst brand in the market, the least known with the smallest market share and minimal functionality and I will outsell you. I will outsell you on Monday, on Tuesday, on Wednesday, on Thursday, on Friday, all next week, this month and next month. I know my product better than you know yours; in fact I know your product better than you do. I know where I am and where I'm going and I never waste my precious time. I will beat you each and every time in every deal. I will always beat you with your big name brand and your big words because I'm better at our job than you are."

Naturally, it's appropriate to keep these thoughts to yourself! Never say it out loud, but always believe your version of this sentiment and back it up with action when thinking about your competition.

Taking this approach doesn't mean blindly ignoring the fact that your competitors' solutions may have their validity. It's more a case of thinking that other solutions may have their attributes, but so does yours and, despite product differences, you're a better sales person and your conduct, sales approach and sales skills will see the customer favor your solution.

Having confidence gets you to the place where you pass the distraction of fear. It means that you're not afraid to:

- Ask the customer for the price you need.
- Hold your price in negotiations.
- Insist that the customer assesses your product demonstration even before you provide a proposal.
- Lose a deal.
- Compete against a solution with superior specifications.
- Cold-call often.
- Self-assess and seek constructive criticism about your sales approach.
- Walk away from time-wasting potential customers.

- Walk away from unprofitable customers.
- Try new sales presentations.
- Forecast future sales honestly.

By taking supreme confidence into the sales field it means you'll not lose your nerve at crunch time during negotiations.

Operate on a different level

You should operate on the basis that you're no longer happy just to be in on the deal; you're not there to 'throw your hat in the ring," to be included as one of three quotes the potential customer is obtaining.

The "be in it to win it" thought process is not the mindset of a professional sales person. You should operate on a different level.

Operating with a full sense of certainty means that you're not just putting on a brave face with your chest puffed out. Your confidence must be *real*. It's more than a positive-can-do attitude. Your confidence must enable you to think and act with utter conviction and clarity of purpose.

Confidence, not arrogance

Naturally you're not better than your employer, your manufacturer, or your brand. This type of thinking is wrong and it's arrogant. However, your performance can and does make all the difference in profitably selling and securing a sales order.

Performing your sales role with complete confidence can see you work with a clear will to win. Everyone wants to win, but having confidence is about your clarity of purpose and your uncompromising will to win.

It becomes a matter of principle to beat your competition. It becomes a matter of principle to obtain the greatest profit level possible in each sale. You're no longer selling for any sales commission or remuneration. You're selling to win and, as with passionate success in any commercial field of endeavor, the money will find you when you concentrate on the right things.

Destroying the seed

How you destroy your seed of doubt is a personal challenge. And it must be destroyed, not merely ignored or suppressed. The method is different for all of us.

You may destroy it because:

- You regularly beat your bigger-named competitor.
- You sell at greater profit levels.
- You're often first place on your sales board.
- You can perform the best demonstration in your branch.
- You always make your sales budget.
- You're simply above it all and don't even take the time to think about such things.

You can destroy your seed of doubt in whatever way you wish. And the sooner the better!

4.2

When on stage

It's a live performance

When you're in front of a potential customer, everything matters.

You're live on stage. There are no second chances, there's no safety net.

Your attention to detail, i.e. how you listen and how you present, are vitally important.

Think about this...

- When your customer greets you in reception, are you lounging in their reception chair, or standing tall ready to greet them?
- What impressions are you creating in front of your customers?
- How natural and sincere does your presentation appear to the customer?
- How knowledgeable and thorough does your customer perceive you to be?

Be charged

You're not an administration or clerical worker who only warms up by the time 10am coffee is available. When you arrive at work you must be prepared and ready to go, whether you're in your office or your customer's office.

In a selling role there's no time to waste getting warmed up after you arrive at work. Do whatever it takes, but when work starts you must be ready to go. Be energetic and enthusiastic!

Stay fresh

There should be no difference between your final sales call of the week at 3pm on Friday afternoon and your first sales call at 9am on Monday morning. Your behaviour shouldn't change all week.

With repetition, assumptions can be easily made because you know what the customer is about to say and you know what you're about to say. You've heard it all before. But remind yourself that your new customer hasn't heard it before. Let them say what they want to say and be enthusiastic about it, despite the fact that you may have seen the show before.

Take your chance

Each sale will have a different tempo and a different breakthrough point with the customer. This is the point when you know that the customer is understanding and appreciating what you've shown and told them.

This will more than likely come when the customer is actively listening and engaged without distraction. You'll notice real progress as they'll be asking spontaneous questions about what you're presenting. And you'll notice your enthusiasm being replicated by the customer.

It may be during a first appointment that it happens and, as a result, your proposal presentation is able to be comparatively brief. You could make the breakthrough during a demonstration meeting. It may be that the customer is engaged and listening when you're in a negotiation appointment. Whenever the time presents itself, take the opportunity and don't rush through the meeting, incorrectly assuming that you'll have the chance to explain things in greater depth at your next meeting.

Circumstances may not present themselves again. Take your chance.

Always be prepared

When the customer is ready to make a decision you could be called in to discuss your proposal at very short notice.

You may have an excellent first appointment, which leads to price discussions, negotiations and even an order being signed. You cannot predict when or what a potential customer may ask you about.

For these reasons you should always have the tools of your trade at every stage of the selling cycle. Be prepared for anything at any time as customers tend to act within their time frame not yours.

4.3

Trust me, I'm a salesman

The expectation from most customers that a sales person is telling "the truth, the whole truth and nothing but the truth" tends to be very low.

It should go without saying that you should always be honest with your customers. Don't promise or imply things if you aren't sure about the answer to a question. Tell the customer that you'll find out and get back to them. Don't guess, or worse, fabricate an answer.

Our approach is often based on telling a story about superior service or product quality and you can only take this approach if it's true and you believe in this for your product.

For some strange reason some sales people are able to justify not presenting with total honesty because, after all, it's business, it's not personal. Don't follow this logic. You'll jeopardize future business with poor ethics.

Some customers aren't always open and honest with sales people either (the "buyers are liars" sentiment is often found within sales departments). But this is no justification to reciprocate. By being open, honest and thorough with your customer you can turn your approach into a competitive advantage because customers generally don't expect it and many of your competitors won't act in the same way.

Punctual, polite and courteous

It may sound obvious, but being sincere, polite and courteous may also give you a competitive advantage. Remember that your customer is a person who wants to deal with someone they feel comfortable with.

Thank the receptionist on the way out. While the receptionist is not typically the decision-maker they can still influence the purchase and provide negative feedback about you if you're perceived as arrogant or impolite.

If you promise to provide more details, make sure you do so and, importantly, do so *when* you say you will. When you're busy each day it's easy to forget a small point or a promised telephone call to a customer. By doing the small things, as you said you would, you instill confidence in your customer and they'll believe that you'll deliver on your larger promises.

Retain confidentiality

Often customers will reveal their future business plans or method of operation during your discussions. Always keep what you know to yourself; never share the information that you've learnt. Don't try to build rapport with other customers in the same industry by using gossip and a lack of integrity.

4·4

You're not alone

Always be part of the team

A sales person's role is typically one of solitude. They're often isolated from their colleagues. So you should always work with your team, despite the healthy competition to out-perform one another each week or month.

It's good to be an individual, but you must be a contributing member of your sales team. Share industry knowledge and experience. Learn from those around you. It's less costly learning from someone else's mistakes than your own.

Knowing how to do something and actually doing it are often two different things. Practice your sales presentations, demonstrations and negotiations with your colleagues. It's less costly making mistakes during practice than doing so with potential customers.

Rehearse with your sales team.

Team selling

Some products lend themselves to breaking the sales process into many parts, involving other sales people, technical and support staff. Team selling can be very powerful as customers will listen to and believe technical people much more than is the case with sales people.

If several people are telling the same story about the company and its products, albeit in a different manner, this can be an unstoppable sales presentation as it's truly comforting to the customer to hear many people saying the same thing to them.

Team selling could involve a sales person and a Sales Manager. It need not be a team of technical or support people. The Sales Manager can have a similar discussion with the customer as the sales person has, but hearing it from two different people tends to increase believability. The risk in this team approach is if the second person's style or sales story is different to the first person's. This will be unsettling to the customer and it may spoil the sales effort, not enhance it.

Team selling is naturally a function of the sales value and complexity of the product. Low value transactions don't warrant two people doing what one person can do, but a team could make all the difference with higher value purchases.

Team selling can be an excellent competitive advantage because it's hard for your competitors to quickly replicate.

4·5

Two golden rules

Always keep two golden rules at the forefront of your actions.

- Rule number one: Follow-up, follow-up, follow-up.
- Rule number two: Never, ever assume anything.

Have a reason to follow them up

Once the selling cycle has commenced you should always have a valid reason for contacting the customer to progress to the next step. If you disclose further relevant information each time you contact the customer they're more likely to take your telephone calls ahead of a competitor who calls "just to see how things are going." It's better if the follow-up calls are perceived as benefiting the customer, as opposed to being of benefit to you.

By working in this way you are again setting yourself apart from your competitors.

Always seek to stay in touch and follow up each and every sales opportunity, regardless of your perception of the opportunity.

Never assume anything

Don't let past experiences, either good or bad, cloud your way of working – always ask your customers the questions you need answers to.

Never make any assumptions about the customer's viewpoint, their needs or values. Ask everything as you work your way through the selling cycle. If you're unsure what their response means, seek clarification. If you don't understand *why* the customer is saying something, ask further questions to clarify.

You should be asking questions at every stage of the selling cycle. Never become lazy by assuming you know what the customer is thinking.

Has anything changed?

Following your first appointment and before any subsequent discussion, always ask, "Has anything changed?"

It's common for the prospect's requirements and expectations to alter throughout the selling cycle as more people within their company have input and they speak to competitor sales people.

Always ask if anything has changed to ensure your discussion is relevant to the prospect's current needs and concerns.

4.6

That's not what I think I said

As you progress through the steps of the sale it's important to be aware of factors relating to how you communicate with your customer.

Communication is about information being exchanged between two people – this isn't necessarily what people are *saying* to each other. Lost sales opportunities often result from poor communication between the customer and sales person. Communication with the customer is an aspect of selling that many sales people don't stop to consider.

The points below aren't presented in any order of importance, but may assist you to assess how you are sending messages to your customer.

First impressions

First impressions always stay with us. They help set the tone of the customer's expectation. Be aware of the initial message you send to your customer in that first meeting.

Most people who are in a sales role can be charming and present well. But you can't rely on the fact that you're a "nice person" to be the reason someone buys from you.

Back up the first impressions you create with informed discussion.

Product knowledge

The easiest way to ensure customers believe that you know what you're talking about is for you to actually know what you're talking about.

Having a detailed knowledge of the finer points of your product, your competitors' products and your industry is at the core of this.

You must be able to speak confidently about your product, after-sales service and payment options. When it comes to product knowledge, don't learn on the job; ensure you have a "pre-season" training run.

Dress for success

Your customer will initially judge you by your appearance and presentation. It's easy to see where people are going by looking at how they're dressed. Ensure that you dress for your market. Don't automatically dress in the stereotypical business suit, unless it's appropriate.

Do you look like you're going to the beach? Or maybe the opera? Perhaps you're going to do some gardening? We can all tell where someone is going by the way they are dressed.

Ensure you dress as someone who is going to be successful.

Repeat, be consistent

Just because you've told the customer about a particular advantage your product has, don't assume that they've heard you the first time, or understood what you meant.

Even if they heard this piece of information there's the added risk that they became confused about which sales person told them what.

At each step of the sale you must reiterate your sales arguments, consistently promoting the same message to the particular customer, emphasizing those points that you know are important to them.

Communicate with who matters

Offer to meet with other decision makers in the customer's company to discuss your proposed solution. If you're not meeting with the key decision maker(s) you're effectively leaving the selling to your contact.

Attempt to meet with the decision makers, even if it means repeating a step of the sale. You may be very good at communicating your sales arguments, but it's of no consequence if you're not talking to the people who sign-off on the deal.

Seeing is believing

Having physical examples, documentation, electronic data and models, written customer references and similar aids within your sales presentation will help the customer to visualize what you're explaining.

A picture may convey in an instant something that could take half an hour to talk about. It has the added benefit of capturing and retaining the customer's interest longer than an extended dialogue.

Incorporating additional resources into your discussions also creates authenticity as it adds to the reality of what the sales person is saying.

Paint the picture

When outlining your sales arguments, draw an analogy with the customer's business. They can relate to their business and their industry but they're often unable to relate to yours. Wherever possible, use examples from their world so they can understand the point you are making.

Less words

Use as few words as possible to present your sales story. Choose your words carefully in order to paint the best image in the customer's mind. For example:

- Say "we" as opposed to "I." "We" refers to you and your company. This has more security than a sales person's individual opinion.
- Say "agreement" as opposed to "contract." Agreements seem more mutually beneficial than contracts. It's acceptable for your customer to discuss your competitor's "contract" but you should always discuss your "agreement."

Don't use industry jargon – terminology you take for granted may have absolutely no meaning to a customer who is not in your industry. By using jargon you risk confusing the customer.

Keep discussions simple and don't get too elaborate with your presentation by adding layers of complexity. The objective should always be for everyone in the room to understand all points being discussed.

Listen more than you talk

By design, you have two ears and one mouth and it's best not to contradict it. You should always listen more than you talk.

Listening is a skill often overlooked. To become effective at listening, the following basic points apply:

- Wait for an answer to your questions.
- Don't talk.
- Don't be thinking of your next sentence.
- Take notes.
- Consider your response to the answers you receive and clarify any uncertain points.
- Maintain eye contact as you listen.
- Don't interrupt the customer when they're speaking, even if you think you're helping. Interrupting is conveying a message to the customer that what you have to say is more important than what they're saying.

By actively listening you're able to locate any hidden agenda the customer may have. You learn a lot about them and this will help you get it right the first time.

If you talk, but don't ask questions or listen properly, you may give the customer an opportunity to disagree with you. You're not guiding the conversation. Your excess comments carry the risk that you could raise concerns in the customer's mind that weren't there to begin with.

Body language is a giveaway

Often it's not *what* the customer is saying, but *how* they're saying it that gives us more information. Watch the customer's body language as it conveys many things.

Factors such as tone of voice, eye contact and physical stance often reveal more than a person intends. When deciding what to do next in a particular sale, ask yourself what's being "communicated", as opposed to what's being said. Where words and actions don't match, your instinct will help you determine the truth of the matter.

Most experienced sales people can "pick up" or "sense" a customer's body language message without being formally educated on what to look for. Often their street-wise intuition is sufficient to understand when what is being said by a customer isn't believable.

Shake hands

Be conscious of the initial hand shake you have when first meeting with a new customer as this can be an early warning signal. In broad terms, the nature of a hand shake often directly relates to the way the sale "plays out" with the customer.

Experienced sales people will have seen those overly strong handshakes where the customer rotates their hand to their left so it's effectively on top of the sales person's hand. Typically this happens with customers who "automatically know more than the sales person." These customers tend to like the sound of their own voice and often don't listen to others, or readily appreciate another person's opinion. They're harder to convince and less likely to be fair and reasonable. They seem to do it their way, regardless of the situation.

The opposite tends to happen when a customer shakes hands in a very light, even limp manner. These sales tend to result in the customer being easily led, but by the last sales person who spoke to them. They can be easily influenced to act in a certain manner. Even worse, they may not take any action or have an influence on the decision.

Not surprisingly, the customers who shake hands in a moderate and considerate manner – where you don't actually notice the nature of their hand shake – are usually those customers who tend to be fair and sensible to deal with. You're able to have fruitful two-way discussions with them and, as a result, they're easier to sell to.

Be observant

In addition to observing a customer's body language, there are other things you might notice that help you better understand them and their business. You just need to be observant.

Here are a few examples:

- The company's "in/out" board at reception may list employee names in order of seniority. This may tell you how relevant your contact is in the decision-making process.
- Notice other visitors in the company's visitor's log. Some older-style visitor books, where companies ask visitors to sign in, allow you to see who's been there before you. You may notice the names of your competitors which will help you tailor your presentation.
- Read company literature while waiting in the reception area. Use the time to assess the size and operation of the company.
- Competitor quotes and brochures are often left about on the customer's desk.
- Walking through the customer's office gives an opportunity to visually assess the tone of the company and gain clues about their priorities and values.

Mimic your customer

Good sales people will naturally mimic their customers without realizing it. They'll automatically match the pace and intensity of discussion to that of their customer.

For example, if the customer is quietly spoken, soft and measured, or appears timid in their discussion, asking questions in a boisterous manner, albeit, enthusiastically, will alienate them. If the sales person speaks in a slow and considerate manner when presenting their sales arguments it will assist them in discussions with this type of customer.

If a customer is time-conscious, professional, factual and exceptionally business-like in their approach, inquiring about their weekend or their pressures at work will not be productive or helpful. A better result will be gained by taking a quick, no-nonsense and direct approach.

Not too smooth

If you're "too smooth" or "too polished" in front of the customer you may appear to be an expert sales person. By having "all the answers" and immediate justifications without reflection may not appear as fantastic as you think it does.

Providing instant answers to all customer objections or queries can in itself create the impression that you're a great "sales person" who has all the answers.

Always be mindful that we're not there to sell the customer on us being a "great sales person." We're there to sell them on the fact that we're an industry expert and the safest option for them to select. Appreciate the difference.

Be different

Be individual in the way you present and in your sales approach. This can set you apart in a positive way. There's little value in being just another version of your competitors. If there's scope for your individuality to shine through, don't hesitate to use it.

4·7

Future sales

Forecasting sales

Knowing what will be sold this month and the following month is an integral business process that enables stock control and helps companies supply services and resources that are necessary in fulfilling customer orders.

If you understand where each of your customers are in the selling cycle, it'll be easy for you to know what orders you'll receive in the current week, as well as the current and subsequent months. By following the steps of the sale and asking questions of your customer, you'll know if it's likely they'll be placing the order with you.

If you're expecting to receive the sales order in the current month then it's a reasonable expectation that you're able to answer the following questions:

- Does the proposed product or solution satisfy all the customer's requirements?
- Does the proposed service solution satisfy the customer's requirements?
- Does the proposed payment method satisfy the customer's requirements?
- Is the customer happy with the proposed expenditure required?

- By when does the customer need to make a decision?
- When is the customer intending to make a decision?
- If not you, what competitor is most likely to receive the order and why?
- Does the customer exclusively make the decision within their organization?
- What is the customer's approval process?

Only when you know the answers to each of the above questions (which you'll establish over the course of the sales steps by asking the right questions and doing your job properly) can you include the customer on a sales forecast list.

Don't guess, pretend or hope to get lucky by confusing a sales forecast list with a wish list. They are two very different things. In business, we don't deal in wish lists!

As always, keep it simple. Your sales forecast is a list of potential sales orders and there's no need to make it any more complicated by documenting the probability in terms of percentages of success for each potential sale.

There's no prize for second place. Whether you are 70% or 99% sure of getting the pending sales order is irrelevant. If you missed out on the sale the end result is the same. If you don't know that you'll be receiving the order then it is a pretty safe bet to assume that you'll not be getting the sale.

Have an electronic or paper list of potential sales and focus your activity on these each month, as this is at the heart of what you do. Not being sure of what you'll sell is not an option. It's also a clear sign that you're not in control of your role or your actions.

What if the sales aren't there?

What if you're in a sales slump and you can't see the potential sales that you expect and need? As you're a human being, not a machine, "the sales slump" is inevitable in the early stages of a sales career.

When confronted with a lack of sales, or potential sales, you need to take a moment or two to reflect on your current predicament.

Initially, look at what you've actually lost and make a clear distinction between potential sales that have been lost and sales that are just delayed and are awaiting buying decisions. Ensure that your sales slump is a reality, not an emotional response to losing a couple of deals that you'd been promised verbally or something similar.

Go back to basics, as your predicament has most likely been caused by you straying from your intended path and plan of action.

You need to:

- Revisit your goals and review what motivates you.
- Check your plan and discover what you've not been doing.
- Review your generic weekly timetable planner and question if you have been following it (see chapter "Our greatest competitor").
- Question your attitude, work ethic and energy level.

The probability is that you've most likely forgotten the basics and lost your clarity of purpose.

If you stick to the basics of the selling cycle, repetitively, consistently – even if at times it may seem boring – and do what you know you should be doing, without distraction, you'll soon be back on track.

Don't take the typical view that your sales slump is because of:

- Lack of marketing / ineffective marketing.
- Lack of market share / market presence.
- High price of your product and service.
- Insufficient product or service capability.

You didn't experience problems with any of these things when you were obtaining sales orders, so they're not a valid factor now.

There are always potential customers out there to sell your product to – you just need to find them!

The rear view mirror

Your slump may not be due to one of the general reasons mentioned above, it may be due to a skill issue, or because you're not doing one step of the sale as consistently or proficiently as you had previously done.

Look back at the last six to twelve months and create a similar matrix as the example that follows. Do this by extracting data from your diary that identifies the amount of lead generation, first appointments, demonstrations, negotiation appointments and orders you've engaged in for each month.

Allowing for time lags, look at the respective ratios between each step of the sale within a given month and compare your higher performance periods to your lower performance periods.

You may notice that most recently you're not doing the appropriate number of first appointments, or that lead generation has fallen. You may discover that you're no longer conducting as many demonstrations as you have previously and this brought you great success.

The ratios between each step of the sale can be measured for each month. The ratios that aren't similar to the months where you had sales success will quickly point you in the direction of the kind of improvement required.

Month	Lead Generation	First Appointment	Demonstration	Negotiation Appointment	Order
August	160	32	8	6	4
July	117	14	6	4	4
June	61	17	6	11	10
May	74	14	7	10	12
April	223	37	22	19	15
March	187	29	16	13	8
February	248	36	19	14	14
January	227	31	18	16	12
December	214	27	17	17	16
November	256	32	15	14	12
October	198	29	16	16	13
September	214	28	14	17	14

The power of common sense

You may not need to go to the extent of assessing your statistics and sales ratios. It may be a matter of keeping things simple. Never underestimate the power of common sense and don't try to be too clever about things.

To restore your confidence, temporarily set aside many of the performance enhancement techniques we've spoken about and get yourself out into the sales field. Talk to, not at, as many potential customers as you can. Get back to basics and build from there.

By concentrating on what *really* matters and what is the most important thing to do will simplify things.

In sales, talking to people who don't currently buy from you is something that needs to be done above everything else. Concentrate on doing this and only this. Then, when you're back on track, start to build your sales skills again.

Take the pressure off yourself. Remind yourself that you don't need to be perfect. You don't need to be the best salesperson in the world. When two people are running from a hungry lion in the jungle they don't need to run at record-breaking speed to be safe; they only need to out-run the person next to them!

In sales it's no different. Understand your sales role for what it is and don't complicate it.

4.8

Overwhelming, yet simple

The customer's perspective

With so many features, advantages and benefits you can identify with your product and an infinite number of ways you could present to a customer within a given sale it's understandable that you can be quickly overwhelmed! To work out the best way forward with a particular customer, look at the sale from their perspective.

Select one main approach to sell to a given customer. Don't try to educate them about all the possibilities you can offer. By listening to your customer as you work your way through your first appointment, the best path to take for that customer will become obvious.

The customer doesn't need to know everything you know about your solution, or your competitive advantages. They only need to know the things that are of interest to them.

Consider this alternative explanation. A man takes his wife out for an evening meal to celebrate her birthday. His wife really enjoyed her meal and when asked why, she was almost lost for words. Was it the taste of the food, the service, or the fact that she didn't have to cook the meal?

Consider a few factors that may have contributed to her enjoyment of the ninety minute meal:

1. Background music.
2. Intimate lighting.

3. Table set perfectly.
4. Table was available when she arrived.
5. Extensive choice of wines.
6. Main course choice was varied.
7. Menu had been tried and tested.
8. Staff trained in attentive but invisible service.
9. Right temperature in dining room.
10. Restaurant was easy to find with convenient parking.

The whole experience was delivered because an extensive amount of thought and preparation went into it. However the customer is only aware of a few key variables, namely the food and possibly the wine menu choices.

The range of variables that contributed to the enjoyment of the evening don't need to enter the customer's mind; the restaurateur is not complicating things by telling the customer about the air-conditioning, the way the menu was designed or other factors.

It's no different in our sales presentations. We may show the customer our "back of house" so they understand the systems and measures the company goes to in order to deliver on its promises, but that doesn't mean that we complicate the delivery of the sales message with non-pertinent details. Make it easy for your customer to decide in your favor by listening to them and considering the sale from their perspective.

The sales person's simplicity

Similarly, in considering the various skills and attributes that an ideal sales person should possess, you can quickly feel overwhelmed if you think there's a need to excel in every one of those skills and attributes.

You may feel the need to excel in certain areas and inadvertently put undue pressure upon yourself.

While we don't advocate mediocrity, keep the level of each skill required for optimal sales success in perspective. A sales person who has a proficient level of skill in each of the disciplines we've touched on in this book will achieve better results than sales people who've attained excellence in any given skill – if this has been attained to the detriment of other skills.

Take, for example, a sales person who has rigorously studied body language and has great communication skills. Their sales results will be deficient if they're unable to generate leads despite the fact that they're a brilliant negotiator.

A sales person who can deliver a fantastic product demonstration in their customer's office on an electronic tablet, but lacks the ability to ask probing questions about the customer's needs may find that their superior presentation skills do not translate to sales success. They may be talking about things that aren't important to their customer.

A blend of proficient level skills will always yield consistent and reliable sales results.

Quick recap: But wait, there's more

Your attitude
As you grow into your sales role you should move beyond simply having a positive outlook in your mental approach; you must tackle your job with utter conviction, clarity and confidence.

Everything matters when you're in front of a customer. There are no "second chances." You need to get it right the first time. The stakes are too high to learn on the job. You're live on stage.

Your ethics
In sales, there are no shades of grey – always be honest and ethical. "Because it's business" is never justification to act inappropriately.

Your golden rules
Always keep two golden rules at the forefront of your actions:

- Rule number one: Follow-up, follow-up, follow-up.
- Rule number two: Never, ever assume anything.

Your communication

Lost sales opportunities often result from poor communication between the customer and sales person. Understand that while communication is about information being exchanged between two people, this isn't necessarily what people are *saying* to each other.

Sales orders are often too easily lost through poor communication. Be clear by using simple words and messages and truly listen to what your customer is saying to you.

Your sales skills

A sales person who has a proficient level of skill in each of the disciplines we've touched on in this book will achieve better results than one who has attained excellence in any given skill, especially if this has been attained to the detriment of other skills.

Your individuality

Be individual in your sales approach as it can set you apart in a positive way. There's little value in being just another version of your competitors. If there's scope for your individuality to shine through, don't hesitate to use it.

But don't forget you're also part of a team. Always contribute as a member of your team; teams often achieve more than individuals.

Stories from the front line

Selling water

Bruce owned the town's fourth-largest spring water company. He started many years ago without a single customer and worked exceptionally hard to get the business to where it is today.

In 17 years, Bruce had seen many a sales person come and go. In fact he gave them little time or courtesy until they could convince him they weren't going to waste either his time or his money.

Bruce was an unemotional boss, always straight to the point, and renowned for his abruptness. Many people thought he was a little too intense and at times even a little rude. Some even suggested that his personality was stolen at birth as all he could talk about was his water company and issues related to his business pursuits. Those work colleagues who did get to know him thought he was a nice guy who was very approachable. They didn't think he was unfair or abrupt, but they had to concede that it was unfortunate that he had an "accountant-like" personality.

The market

Bruce's company had about 14 competitors in town, also selling water to households. He specialized in those large 5 gallon bottles that sit upside down on a refrigeration dispenser.

In addition to directly competing with others selling the same bottled water door-to-door, Bruce had a number of indirect competitors. Some sold crates of small pack, personal-sized water bottles, while many sold water purifying systems to attach to a household tap. Customers could also choose to purchase similar products from their mall or even enjoy free water from their kitchen tap. It was a crowded market but it was large enough for those willing to work.

Bruce employed six sales people to cover their town. Their salary was 100% commission for sales achieved. Sales people only received their commission after the customers had paid the company. Bruce was very "old school" so the sales people were left to their own devices and didn't have sales territories to work within. They were free to sell anywhere in town, even if they were competing against each other. Bruce's attitude was if they were stupid enough to compete with each other and waste their time in doing so, then it should cost *them* money, not him.

The business philosophy

Bruce's philosophy was simple. His sales people should cold-call door-to-door and work hard. He didn't really understand computers, or even know what marketing was. To him, these were elaborate things created by someone with too much time on their hands to substitute for common sense. Bruce was not a fan of electronic databases or advertising flyers or any such things. To him, these things all seemed to make life harder and more complicated.

Bruce simply sold water. Everyone needed water to live, so the sales people should go and ask people if they would like to buy some. If they don't want to buy water, just ask someone else. It was a no-fuss, clear and simple approach that had worked very well for 17 years and no one was ever going to prove to Bruce anything to the contrary. Sales people were free to conduct their role in whatever way they saw fit. Bruce would not intervene.

Star performers

Bruce had two star sales people who stood the test of time, having been with him for almost five years. They were at the "opposite ends of the earth" in terms of their sales approach. Louis and Frederick were excellent income earners for Bruce's company and for themselves, but they had vastly different ways of working and of looking at the world.

Louis was in every way an ordinary person. He was not particularly athletic; some thought he was a little too short to be a successful sales person. He was of average ability and it was fair to say that he was not the most formally-educated. Louis wore a white shirt, trousers and a colorful tie to work each day. If it was cold he may wear his tweed jacket. But only if it was cold. He drove a modest but presentable and reliable vehicle that he'd bought with cash.

Louis's tastes were simple. He didn't want for the finer things in life and he certainly wasn't the life and soul of any party. Louis spoke with a country accent that sounded like it belonged in a cowboy movie. He did, however, have a sense of humor. Louis would often joke with the girls in the order processing department when they poked fun at him. He would say that although he was short, he considered himself lucky that his legs still reached the ground. More than once a week he proudly said to the girls, "'trust me, I'm a salesman." This was his standard joke, but they continued to enjoy it in good humor.

Frederick was everything his three syllable name implied. He was eloquent, charming and well-versed in his use of the Queen's English. Frederick was tall, thin and would only ever be seen wearing his suit. He always wore a tailored black or black pin stripe suit and a pristine double-cuff shirt, complete with gold cufflinks. His Italian silk ties were mostly red.

Frederick was confident and possibly a little too outwardly confident. He always drove the most expensive vehicle that he could afford to finance. Frederick constantly read sales books to improve his skills. He was career-driven and results-oriented. He was loved by his customers, but less so by the order processing girls as he was sometimes perceived as being a little condescending towards them.

Differing styles

Louis and Frederick set about their tasks in completely different ways. Louis's business card referred to him as a "'Sales Person," while Frederick called himself an "Account Consultant." Louis wrote his orders out with a 15 cent blue plastic pen but Frederick would not be seen without the expensive High Street pen he referred to as his "writing instrument."

Louis did not operate an electronic database; he only kept a simple record of the part of town he was due to call, to help him keep a regular calling pattern. He didn't send flyers to potential customers announcing his arrival in their area on a certain day, unlike Frederick who did this meticulously.

Frederick also created visiting flyers to leave with potential customers if he was unsuccessful on a sales call. Louis left only his business card. He figured he would be calling again on that same door soon, so providing a flyer was a waste of money and effort. Louis worked solo, but Frederick employed a sales secretary to administer his database, send advertising flyers and conduct telemarketing calls.

It's all in the work

Both Louis and Fredrick worked long hours each day. They would arrive at the office at 7am and leave the office at 6pm each working day. Louis left the office every day at 8am and headed out into the field to cold-call. Regardless of what part of town he was in, he would not stop knocking on doors until 4.30pm each afternoon. He would then return to the office to hand in his orders and then check and respond to emails.

Frederick, on the other hand, usually had more important tasks to execute each morning before he headed out to the sales field. He may have to meet with the Logistics Manager about an issue he was aware of, or meet with his IT computer consultant, or spend time planning his advertising flyer for the following month. Often it was 10 or 11 am before he was able to leave the office. Routinely, Frederick would return to the office around 3pm to follow through on various issues. He would write long emails to the Logistics Manager if he discovered a dissatisfied customer during the day. He would blind copy Bruce on the email. He would write a detailed message outlining the issue and was always sure to explain how a dissatisfied customer has a negative impact on the conduct of business.

Often, Frederick's emails would be followed by a visit to Bruce to explain it in person. Sometimes Frederick would start writing these messages on his cell phone while he was in the field.

Louis had a different perspective on customer complaints about the Logistics department. He would apologize to the customer, telephone the Logistics Manager and leave it with him. He doubted that Bruce knew how to turn on his computer, let alone read an email. Louis figured that the Logistics Manager would fix the issue if he brought it to his attention. Louis would call the customer three days later to ensure they were happy and leave things at that.

Frederick would often take customers out for lunch or to play golf. He also spent time at monthly meetings and lunches held by the industry associations and the local business networking chapter. Frederick knew the importance of having a profile in the community.

A local cable TV station was doing a story on the water industry and they asked both Louis and Frederick to be interviewed. Frederick jumped at the chance to increase his profile, but Louis was skeptical that his comments would be edited and the actual benefit of wasting a morning filming would not be realized. Louis never conducted corporate golf days or attended industry association functions. As far as he was concerned, no one there was going to buy water from him, so what was the point?

Selling perspectives
Frederick believed that selling was about having a relationship, whereas Louis thought selling was about "'selling something." He didn't want a

relationship; he just wanted to sell water then move to the next customer. Louis would knock on a door and say, "Hi, I'm here to see if you like water?" From there, he would have a normal discussion with the potential customer. Louis would sometimes relate a story about water quality that he experienced growing up on a farm, but generally he wouldn't entertain the idea of being too technical or too dramatic.

Louis always set his cell phone to beep 15 minutes after he sat down with a customer. This reminded him that it was time to move on to the next customer. On the other hand, Frederick had charts, research statistics and water samples that he carried with him everywhere. When a customer would open the door he would start by saying, "Hi, I'm here to warn you about the quality of the water you're drinking." Once seated, he would execute a long and detailed sales presentation, surrounded by facts, figures, charts and samples. At times, his presentation was so alarming that a customer would insist that their first delivery be on that same day.

Frederick always targeted the more luxurious parts of town as he figured that they had the most money to spend. He also enjoyed the more opulent surroundings! Louis would never target the luxury suburbs as, in his experience, these people always wanted to spend too long speaking to you and they tended to be an expert on everything. Louis much preferred condominiums and high-rise apartment blocks as he could cover many doors quickly. Time wasn't wasted getting in and out of his car all day.

Louis would stop for lunch which he brought with him from home every day. Aside from thinking this more economical, his real reason was that he didn't need to waste time waiting in lunch bars and cafes. He would eat his lunch, return any phone messages he'd received in the morning and call his wife for a few minutes to see how her day was going. After 15 or so minutes, Louis was back on task knocking on doors. He couldn't see the point in waiting around.

Frederick thought it was "lower-class" to bring your lunch from home. He felt he was entitled to relax for 30 minutes and have lunch in a nice cafe. After all, he did work long hours each day, so some balance in the day was a good thing.

Edward the trainee

Bruce asked Louis to take young Edward into the field and show him the ropes. Trainee sales people were always sent out with Louis. Frederick would not have them as he said they cramped his style and sent the wrong message to his customers. Frederick really feared growing a competitor who may someday show him up!

Louis was happy to have trainees learn from him, but his approach was very low-key. Edward followed Louis around for two full days and Louis spoke very little. Edward impressed Louis, as he didn't complain about constantly working and walking everywhere as previous trainees had. The questions he asked were relevant and well-considered. Edward, like Louis, didn't talk for the sake of hearing his own voice. Edward had impressed Louis, so, on the third day at lunchtime Louis sat him down and gave him some advice.

"Listen kid, I'm only going to tell you this once. Take what you want from it, but we haven't got time to waste." Edward feared Louis was about to tell him the world was about to end, but also sensed the sincerity in Louis's voice.

"You wanna be good at sales? Well here it is and listen fast," Louis told him.

"The sales field is a great leveler. The "wanna-be's" and the "gonna's" all fail out on the street. Out here it's not about your Ivy League education, who you know, who you pretend to be, or how much money you think you have. The street will eat you up if you're a pretender. It's all about common sense and action, not theory. Some days you can walk through brick walls. Other days you may lie in bed curled in a ball not wanting to get out and face the real world. That's normal, that's sales and it never changes. You need to believe in yourself. No one else will if you don't."

Technique is everything

"Being successful in sales is all about your technique," Louis continued to a puzzled Edward. He hadn't noticed any "'technique" after almost three days with Louis. He interrupted and asked for clarification.

"Technique is everything, kid." Louis knew that Edward spent most nights working out at his local health club.

"You ever watch the Olympics, kid? Take a look at those skinny thin guys in the weight-lifting. They look like nothing at all and can lift unbelievable amounts of weight above their head in a single movement. Then look at all those bigger guys at the gym tonight. Ninety-five percent of these guys at every gym around the country can't lift half as much as those slim guys in the low weight divisions at the Olympics."

"Apart from the fact that your gym buddies spend most of their time looking at themselves in the mirror instead of working out, the reason they're not as good is their technique. Most of them don't know how to lift correctly. They think they do, but they don't. The guys at the Olympics have been trained to lift in the correct manner and that makes all the difference. It's all in their technique. They get the most out of the situation because they do things in the right order and in the right way, consistently without distraction and without compromise."

"So what's your sales technique?" asked Edward innocently.

"It's simple:

1. Everything is competitive, but the opportunity is enormous. You can't possibly avail yourself of all the opportunity. Never forget that and never, ever waste time talking about either point.
2. The bread ain't gonna swim to the ducks! They have to swim to it, which is why they have legs. Once they understand that, they stop eating stale bread and go get themselves a fresh loaf! Got it?
3. We're here to work, not be sociable. Customers are customers, not my friends. I socialize on the weekend and don't waste time during selling hours.

4. Big words scare me and I'm not alone in this regard. So never use them.
5. Concentrate on today's game. The season will take care of itself if you win each week's game.
6. It's not about who is better, it's about getting the order. Let customers think they are superior to you if they want to, but get the order and leave your ego at home."

"That's a technique?" queried Edward.

"Yes kid, I see things in simple terms and I just do it. I never get distracted or concerned about people who make things harder than they need to be. It works for me. Others do things differently and it may work for them, but know who you are and what the best technique is for what you want to achieve and then stick to it! Things are that simple."

"When I get rejected at a door I smile, thank them and get on to the next one without prejudice. I know that when I knock on that same door in 58 days time there could be a new householder there, or they may have just had a baby so their priorities have changed. They might have seen something on a day time talk show or whatever, who cares. But when I knock that second time there is a good chance they won't be rude, but actually thank me for coming as they were getting around to calling a company like ours."

The penny was starting to drop for Edward. But just as he was starting to enjoy this lesson in the afternoon sun, Louis said it was time to go. He pointed him towards the opposite building, indicating that he should go and start work on his own. "Off you go, actions are always better than words," said Louis.

Your escalator speed

"Oh and one more thing kid, always watch your escalator speed. It's critical," said Louis.

"Escalator?" said Edward

"You know, moving stairs," clarified Louis.

"What do you mean?" asked a bemused Edward.

"It's a common theory, kid. In Shanghai and in Hong Kong the escalators move fast, very fast. Double the speed they do around here. Why? Because there are a lot of folk there and it's a competitive world. Slow is not an option, things have to be fast if they're going to work. In our local mall the escalator speed is slow and deliberate, in line with the local folks' mindset and the speed restrictions imposed by our public liability insurance companies."

"Regardless of those around you, always have a fast escalator speed. Don't slow down to the speed of others. Got it?"

Louis walked back towards his building, shouting one last word of advice over his shoulder.

"Remember kid, it's only water. Sink or swim. It's your choice kid, no one else's."

Louis or Frederick?

Edward made a great attempt for the remainder of the afternoon. As he called door-to-door, he couldn't help hearing Louis's comments replaying in his mind. He still had one niggling question, as it all seemed too simple to him. He'd heard about and seen the success Frederick had achieved. He looked accomplished and experienced. Yet his approach seemed so different. Who was right, Louis or Frederick?

Edward returned to the office and submitted his first order without any fuss or acclaim. He then paid a visit to the company's Financial Controller to see if she could shed some light on who had the better approach, Louis or Frederick.

Evelyn, the Financial Controller was only too willing to help young Edward on the right path. Edward explained what he had seen and asked if Evelyn would explain which sales person was the better performer. Evelyn could not break confidentiality but confided that by far both Frederick and Louis were the most successful and consistently performing sales people the company had seen in 15 years. Both had personal incomes that exceeded any other company employee by over 50%.

Evelyn explained that Louis and Frederick often had similar monthly results, but on an annual basis, Louis always sells about 20% more units than Frederick. Evelyn went on to say that Louis tended to sell units with 15% more gross profit than Frederick. Suddenly it all became clear to Edward which approach would be more beneficial to him.

Truth be told, Edward was glad to establish that Louis's approach would work for him. He didn't want to have to worry about computers and marketing flyers and he certainly didn't have the money to employ a sales secretary. He was glad that he could concentrate on doing his job as simply as possible in order to succeed.

As Edward was leaving Evelyn's office she said, "Oh and Frederick takes two weeks annual leave a year, one at Thanksgiving and one week at Christmas, but Louis takes 8 continuous weeks leave each year. He negotiated this with Bruce. Every year, he takes his three children to Disneyland for three weeks and then onto Hawaii for five weeks for an extended beachside holiday."

Part 5: Selling for profit

By design, we've left this chapter until one of the last. If you practice the approach we've discussed already you'll invariably find that the customer has already understood why you charge what you charge. Following the steps of the sale we've outlined will help ensure that price is probably the customer's fourth or fifth factor in their decision making, not the first.

If you're presenting a story from the first appointment that's based on you being different to your competitors, with a sales story that promotes a quality solution, the customer will understand what to expect from you by the time you provide the proposal, including pricing.

If your proposed expenditure is not significantly greater than your competitors (as the customer often expects, given the quality and professionalism of your conduct and presentation) then you've completely removed your competitor from the buying equation and you're able to sell your product or solution at healthy and profitable price points.

We can't present a similar sales story as our competitor and then, at the end of the selling cycle, expect the customer to pay us more, just for dealing with us.

Selling for profit is all about how you conduct all of the steps of the sale. It starts with your performance and presentation when you first meet the customer. We need to sell a consistent message throughout the steps of the sale in order for the customer to appreciate that quality, security and value-for-money may have a higher initial dollar cost than a competitor's solution.

Selling for profit is only partly related to holding your price in a price negotiation when the customer is seeking a discount (see "Let's talk" in Part 2). Selling for profit is actually about selling for the price that you want, or need, to sell at in order to deliver the appropriate re-muneration to you and your organization.

In addition to understanding what we've outlined above, we've listed below a series of small points – in no particular order of importance – that may also be useful in ensuring that you retain your sales margin and sell for profit.

Stay in control

At times you need to be strong when leading the customer through the steps of the sale – in order to do what's best for you.

For example:

- Following a first appointment, the customer asks you to email your proposal and doesn't want to meet with you.
- The customer asks that you provide a written quotation at your first appointment.
- The customer requests a written proposal before they attend a demonstration of your product.

These examples move control from the sales person to the customer. It's important to negotiate to do things in the order that will be of most benefit to you.

By providing a quote at a first appointment, based on the theory that "you have to be in it to win it," is like a decision to play lottery; it's not about selling properly. The "you have to be in it to win it" mentality sells products for your competitor, not you. You're not there to help the customer justify the purchase of your competitor's product.

If the customer will not agree to meet with you, they're not serious about working with you. Providing a proposal is not a matter of customer service. If you're not going to sell something, walk away from unreasonable customers and don't waste your time.

The "profit is good" mindset

Never make excuses for making a profit. This is the reason business exists.

The customer is also in business and they too should understand the need to make profit. You must make profit so you can continue to be of service to your customer. If questioned by a customer simply explain, "Mr.(s) Name we need to make a profit so we can continue to be of service to you."

You can't afford to feel that you're taking advantage of your customer if you're able to secure a higher profit margin in sales orders. Our role, the game we are in, is to transfer profit from other organizations to ours. In business-to-business direct selling we're not in a market where we're taking advantage of "mom and pop" domestic consumers. Profit is a good thing and a healthy objective.

Sales people worry most about price

Concern over the selling price being proposed is usually a problem in the sales person's mind long before it enters a customer's mind. Because some sales people have lost business in the past to lower-priced competitors, they tend to think that price is the most important issue for the customer, when it probably isn't.

If having a low price point was the asset many sales people believe, we should see the cheapest, lowest-priced supplier dominate the marketplace with at least 70% of the market. Think of your own market. There's a strong likelihood that the supplier with the reputation for the lowest price point may have one of the smaller market shares by units sold; they're not likely to be dominating your market place.

Think of your product price book (for those sales people who have product pricing flexibility at the sales person level). Typically you take your lowest sell-base price and add a margin that you're comfortable selling at.

For example, if the lowest sell-base price of your product is $10 000 then you might be content to sell to the customer at $12 800. Next week your supplier changes the lowest sell-base price to $11 850. You're comfortable with a sales margin of $2 800 so now you take a price to your next customer of $14 650. You have no problem asking for $14 650 as you're comfortable with your $2 800 sales margin.

Why do you need to wait for your manufacturer to increase the price? You don't. The customer doesn't know your lowest sell-base price, only you do. There's no logical reason to gravitate to the lowest sell-base price and you should always try to avoid doing so.

Pick any two
Which of these points are you promoting with your sales story?

- Cheapest price.
- Service and after-sales service.
- Quality product.

All business people and even domestic consumers understand that you can't have all three. You can only have any two of the three points.

How can you say to your customer with any sense of credibility that you have the best quality product, the most reliable after-sales service and the cheapest price? How can you credibly say to your customer that you're better than your competitor if you cost the same or less? Quality and reliability always cost more, regardless of the type of product or service.

No reason for no profit
There is no acceptable business reason to make a sale without making a profit. Why should you sell something and make a loss or break even? It doesn't make business sense.

Some sales people will take an order for little return, based on their perception that it will lead to future business. This rarely happens as the precedent and expectation of low price points has been set. You can't put the promise of a future sale in your bank. Turnover does not pay the bills. This can only be achieved through sales margin and gross profit.

Sales people selling to major accounts with high volume sales often don't expect to make much money despite the number of units they will sell in a given order. When securing the business of a major account many suppliers may even seek the business at price points below cost. This is generally a symptom of poor sales management and poor sales skills.

If you're selling to a national bank, mining company, national law firm, ask yourself whether they sell to their customers at price points that are below their operating costs? Do your major account customers do business with their customers even if it costs them money to do so? No they don't, or they wouldn't continue to be in business.

By definition, a sales person sells products and services for a profit. If you engage in selling at breakeven price points, or below the direct cost to provide the product or service, this is not selling. It's "giving away" or even charity. To sell for profit you must have the right attitude.

Lifespan pricing

It's often helpful to consider the lifespan of your product and divide that period of time into its selling price. This enables you to talk about an effective cost per day, week, month or year, whichever makes most sense for your product. Talking about the smaller amounts of customer expenditure helps to paint a better picture of the value you're providing.

Price is not what people buy

The price is what it costs for a customer to get what they want. Customers don't buy a price.

Let's say you go to the shopping mall to buy a new shirt. You look at all the casual shirts that you're interested in. Then you narrow it down to styles and colors you like. You then select styles with long sleeves without a button down collar. Your choice is narrowed to two after trying them on and comparing how they fit. Finally you look at the price and justify to yourself why you should pay what you need to in order to wear the shirt you most prefer.

You didn't go into the mall with firm dollar expenditure in mind. You didn't automatically take out all the $50 shirts and then start to narrow your choice down on that basis.

Rather, you had a need and an idea about the type of shirt you wanted and when you found it you were prepared to spend $90 because of how it looked and felt when you tried it on. Your customer has a similar approach.

Aim high

If you have any doubt about where to position your price for a particular customer always start high. Don't start low.

If you've misread the situation and the customer does want to deal with you, then it's very difficult to increase price points. If in doubt, start high as it's easy to decrease your asking price, much harder to increase it.

Talk value-for-money

Throughout the steps of the sale you should think and talk in terms of value-for-money. You should be positioning your solution as the best value-for-money, given the quality and reliability it provides.

For example, "Mr.(s) potential customer, are you going to make your decision based on which option is the lowest price or the best value-for-money?"

When price is the issue

Price generally becomes a major part of the decision process when the customer sees little or no difference between the available options, or appreciates that there is a difference, but places little value on it.

This usually happens when the sales person has done a poor job, the customer has not understood or grasped the issues explained to them, or the sales person wasn't given the opportunity to do their job properly as they were unable to sell to the decision maker(s).

If the customer needs to use a spreadsheet to help them make their decision, your sale is likely to be lost. Product specifications will likely even out across competing products and the lowest price will typically win because a spreadsheet may not capture:

- Reliability of a product or solution.
- How honest the sales person is.
- Value-for-money.
- Market reputation of the supplier.
- Quality characteristics.

Decisions made without common sense will always be hard to combat.

See things in context
Don't get caught up in micro thinking when deciding the price you're going to propose, or when you find yourself in price negotiations with your customer.

In the context of your customer's total business costs the price of your product may not be a great deal of money. Be realistic and see things in context. See them for what they are for your customer. Don't use your industry for perspective.

Always sell the difference
You're not there to justify why the customer should be spending say, $1 400 per month. You're there to justify why they should spend the extra amount say, $350, which is more than their current expenditure.

We're selling the benefits they'll enjoy by dealing with us and switching to our solution.

The cost of these extra benefits is the additional amount they'll pay compared to their current expenditure. This is the equation in most customers' minds and if it's not, it's your job to put it there. It's easier to sell a smaller amount of expenditure. Justify the additional expenditure that's required.

The same applies when a customer expects to enjoy your solutions at the same, lower cost offered by your competitor. You need to sell the difference between your price and your competitor's price.

Calculating your margin

If you have flexibility to create end-user pricing and you want to sell at a 30% gross margin, be sure to do your calculations as outlined in Example A below. Don't calculate using Example B.

Calculating your sales margin based on Example A provides greater margin. More importantly, the main reason for this approach is to allow us to slightly discount our proposed price during negotiations, should this be needed. We'll then know where we are in terms of sales margin after the discount is applied.

If we discount 5% in Example A without calculations we still know we have 25% margin in the deal. If we discount 5% in example B, it will be less attractive to the potential customer and we've lost 21% of the margin we had and will only have 19% margin in the deal.

	Example A	Example B
Base Price = $6,000	Divide by .7	Add 30%
Initial Sell Price	$8 571	$7 800
Initial Sales Margin	$2 571	$1 800
Margin as % of turnover	30%	23%
New Sell Price after 5% discount	$8 142	$7 410
New Margin	$2 142	$1 410

New Margin as a % of turnover	26%	19%
Sales Margin Lost	$429	$390
% Sales Margin Lost	17%	21%

Assumptions cost you the most

Let's assume your potential customer told you who your two competitors were in this particular deal. Based on their market reputation and your experience you know they are generally cheap, very cheap. So you maximize your chance of success by providing your quote with a much lower sales margin than your usual margin.

You rationalize that some return is better than nothing. After presenting your proposal, to your surprise the customer confirms that you are the cheapest quote they've received.

The problem is that when you heard the name of your competitor you assumed they proposed a cheap price. An inexperienced competitor sales person may have proposed pricing on an over-specified product, i.e. a product which was too large and highly optioned for the potential customer's needs, resulting in a higher priced quote.

Assumptions always cost you money, so avoid them. In sales, never assume anything. Always ask your customer what you need to know.

Proactively discount

The longer a potential sale takes, the higher the risk of greater competition. At times it may help to give your customer an incentive to make the buying decision sooner than they had anticipated making the decision.

You could offer any type of financial incentive or benefit to the customer, but plan this approach carefully in advance to ensure you don't jeopardize your sales margin. This can be an appropriate way to reduce the amount of your time needed to obtain the order, as well as beating your competitor.

Before taking this approach, consider the following:

- Ensure the customer is able to proceed with placing the order.
- The incentive needs to be realistic as you may lose credibility if you suddenly discount large amounts.
- The incentive has to be relevant to the customer's actual needs. It needs to be something they'll value.
- You must present your offer with a deadline, rather than presenting an open-ended offer. Creating a deadline reduces the likelihood of your competitor also being consulted.
- Discounting doesn't substitute the need to follow the steps of the sale as we need the customer to prefer our solution first and want to deal with us.

When you proactively discount, the customer usually doesn't think to ask for additional incentives as you're still in control of the sale.

Ask for the order

When the time is right, ask if you can proceed. Don't encourage the customer to procrastinate further. If they don't want to proceed, ask what the issue is and solve the objection or concern as quickly as you can.

"Can we proceed?", "Are there any other issues we need to cover off before we process the order?", "Are you happy that we organize delivery?" There are many ways you can suggest to the customer that it's time to place their sales order. By doing so, you'll receive more orders than you anticipate, or you'll be able to truly establish where they're in at in terms of their desire to order from you.

Always be yourself

In negotiating to hold price it doesn't mean that it's time to become a hard-nosed and steely-faced business person. Ensure that you retain your personality when negotiating.

If the customer asks you to "look at changing the price" then tell them that you would feel bad charging them more, but you'll do so if they want! Don't change your style, or become panic-stricken simply because the order is in sight. Always be yourself, whatever selling stage you're in.

Change what you sell them

If you're discussing a customer concern over your price you might want to revisit the product type that you've quoted them and suggest alternative products to better accommodate their budget.

Mostly you'll see that the customer is willing to work out a way forward. You'll be surprised how often this approach works for you and the customer.

Start at the right selling price

When deciding what selling price to quote a particular customer (should you have flexibility), you should select the right price to start with, based on:

- What level of control in the sale you have with this customer.
- The competitors you have on this deal.
- The amount of time you've devoted to the deal.
- Your perception of the customer's attitude toward quality – based on the products and suppliers you've observed at their business.

It's good to charge more than most of your competitors, but you can't be double or triple the cost of your nearest competitor. Start with a price that's appropriate for the circumstances.

Sell payment by installments

Payment or finance acquisition methods will vary in name and structure across products and industries, but, where possible, offer payment by installments as this is always easier to sell.

This doesn't imply that your company must carry the customer's extended payment terms. There are many financiers who can provide finance arrangements to ensure your company immediately receives full payment upon delivery and enables the customer to pay for a product over the period of use.

Buying signal = no discount

If the customer asks about product availability, delivery or implementation lead time, this generally tells you that they see themselves with your solution. It's pointless discounting when you hear these questions. Notice these obvious buying signals and believe them.

If they're taking the time to ask about price, in most cases, they want your product.

Ensure that you don't give away price if you can see that you're the preferred option.

Every little bit counts

Don't "throw" anything in when doing the deal unless you have to. Small amounts over lots of customers soon add up. Don't give away the little extras, such as delivery, set-up, or establishment fees.

Let's say you manage to charge your customer the small fees associated with set-up or installation only four times per month. Annually, a small charge of say, $140 per sale will equate to $6 700 extra sales margin that you have achieved ($140 x 4 = $560 x 12 months = $6 700).

Small amounts aren't big costs to customers so they're easily sold and passed on. Yet small amounts add up to notable amounts for the supplier and for you!

No control = no profit

If you don't have control throughout the process and you're reacting to the customer's demands you can't expect to secure the order, let alone secure a profitable order.

If you're not dealing with the decision-maker you have very little control. Where possible, always seek to meet with the decision-maker.

Don't be distracted

You may have many products. At times, the excitement of new product lines can be distracting and appear to present great sales opportunities. Be sure to spend your precious time pursuing customers who'll purchase the products or services that are the most profitable to you and your company. There's no point concentrating on selling products that have a poor return for the time you invest.

Always promote all of your products on all sales calls, but only actively pursue sales of products that remunerate the company – and yourself – the most.

Ask for objections

Ask the customer what they think of your proposed solution, price, service support, etc. Ask the customer how they're going to assess their options. What will factor in their decisions? Don't be afraid to ask what some sales people wrongly call, "the hard questions."

Encourage and ask for objections. Talk about any fine print that you may have in your proposal or agreements. If you don't, your competitors will. By doing this, you're leaving nothing to chance.

Protect your time

When you have a customer who genuinely suggests that price is the only issue, do the right thing, but only do what you have to do for that customer. Don't waste any further time.

If you have few customers in your sales pipeline then you'll be reluctant to move on. It's costly to waste time on a potential customer whom you know you're unable to succeed with if you could be spending the time looking for profitable customers.

Have different profit expectations

Match your expected profit return to each situation, i.e. based on the level of control you have in a given sale and the nature of the customer. The more time you spend pursuing the customer, the more sales margin and profit you should desire.

If you've been unable to impress the customer, or haven't had the opportunity to sell to them as much as you felt you needed to, then have lower expectations of profit. Some profit is better than no profit.

It's crucial not to lower your expectations for all sales and always start high. Only adjust your expectations when you have to and assess each sale in isolation.

Don't let a lower expectation of smaller returns become the norm for you.

Don't always have immediate answers

The more selling time you have in front of the customer, the greater the chance you have of "breaking through." On some occasions you may be "breaking through" to first place, but may not yet be ahead of all of your competitors.

For example, you may know that the customer is seeing another one or two of your competitors the day after your visit. Let's say the customer wanted some more information from you or even some product samples. Instead of taking the samples out of your briefcase immediately, arrange to drop in with them the day after next when you're in the area. This provides another selling opportunity for you with the customer. Better still, you're now able to establish how the customer went with their other meetings.

By being a little strategic you can retain control of the sale.

Slow economy can still mean profitable sales

When the economy is in a downturn and businesses behave cautious-ly, don't make the assumption that this implies automatic favor to the cheapest solution available.

In periods when businesses exercise more caution about their expenditure, they're also more cautious about making a wrong decision as it will cost them even more to rectify this.

If you sell a secure and thorough solution based on value-for-money, you'll find that, relative to the decline in the size of the market, you may not experience a proportionate decline in your sales.

Success leads to success

When you confidently sell and surpass your monthly sales budget you've created a choice for yourself in the way that you view those marginal deals you're still working on.

Marginal deals are those where you don't have full control but you may be able to secure the order at lower profit margins than you would normally desire. You can choose to walk away, as you have the luxury of not needing to waste your time pursing the less profitable deals. After all, you've already achieved your monthly sales budget.

Alternatively, you may decide to collect on those marginal deals, take reduced profit (not nil profit) and obtain the order so you can de-motivate your competitors.

This choice of doing marginal business is only possible if you maintain your standards and firstly achieve your sales budget profitably. Don't let a "win at all costs" mentality become your benchmark.

The whites of their eyes

Always try to meet in person with your customer. To better understand what the customer is thinking you need to be able to see their eyes. This is the best way to judge the reality of the situation. It's difficult to sell profitably over the telephone or electronically via email or similar.

Avoid the temptation to email your proposal. By presenting a hard copy proposal in person you have the opportunity to take your customer through it and verify that they understand it. You also have the opportunity to read their body language and ask for feedback on your product, service systems and proposed finance method.

No excuses

We can do all of the above when the situation arises, but a key factor in your ability to charge a customer what you need to charge them is this – you must have the confidence to ask them to pay what they need to pay.

You must deliver yourself without hesitation; a certainty must permeate your sales discussions to the extent that it's "an assumption that the price is what it is." You conduct the sale in the way that it's not and never was an expectation that price would or should be discussed. By conducting the sale with this attitude, you'll appreciate that the above is easy to do and you'll be successful on your terms. After all, this is what it's all about.

Quick recap: Selling for profit

Your profit

Selling for profit is about selling for the price you want or need to deliver the appropriate remuneration to you and your organization.

You can't afford to feel that you're taking advantage of your customer if you're able to secure a higher profit margin in sales orders. Your role is to transfer profit from other organizations to yours. Profit is a good thing and a healthy objective.

Your message

Selling for profit is about how you conduct all of the steps of the sale, starting with your performance and presentation when you first meet the customer.

You need to sell a consistent message throughout the steps of the sale in order for the customer to appreciate that quality, security and value-for-money may have a higher initial dollar cost than a competitor's solution.

Remember that you're selling the benefits they'll enjoy by dealing with your company and switching to your solution.

The cost of these extra benefits is the additional amount they'll pay compared to their current expenditure. This is the equation in most customers' minds and if it's not, it's your job to put it there.

Your profitable products

Always promote all of your products on sales calls, but only actively pursue sales of products that remunerate the company – and yourself – the most.

And be sure to spend your precious time pursuing customers who'll purchase the products or services that are the most profitable to you and your company.

It's good to charge more than most of your competitors, but you can't be double or triple the cost of your nearest competitor. Start with a price that's appropriate for the circumstances.

Part 6: Action time

It's now time to act.

Don't procrastinate, over-analyze, contemplate, question, seek more product knowledge, reassess or make anything more difficult than it need be.

Actions are all that matter.

Concentrate your time and energy on what matters and eliminate all else from your schedule and your thoughts.

Create a simple road map and hit the road in the full understanding of what really matters. Appreciate that the only factor that may limit your success is common to all of us – lack of time.

In this part:
A small and deliberate action plan
Our greatest competitor

6.1

A small and deliberate action plan

Working to a plan

Whether you're new to the role or an experienced sales person, it pays to work in an organized and focused manner. To be continually successful you need to be balanced in your use of time.

If you spend all your time following up current customers at the expense of lead generation you'll undoubtedly hit a sales slump because you neglected to spend enough time looking for new ones. You can't be too busy to learn about a new product your company has just introduced or you may miss valuable sales opportunities.

With so many demands on your time you need a simple plan to keep you on course and ensure that you don't get distracted or miss opportunities. A plan helps you to stay focused, to be organized and, as a consequence, be consistently successful.

Don't be fearful about the complexity or the time involved in documenting a working plan (or action plan). In its simplest form it's basically a "to do" list.

Houses don't "just get built." There is a plan and a series of steps that must be followed in order to build the house. A house may still be built without a plan, but it may take longer, cost more, be unsafe to live in and not present as impressively as intended.

A cross-country road trip to a given destination is quicker, more cost effective and less stressful, if you follow directions. When it comes to building your sales career, having a plan or road map has the same role in your success as it does for the traveler on a road trip and the builder of a house. The value of a plan can't be disputed.

In a previous chapter we took time to think about big picture goals to help us clarify our motivation. Now we turn our attention to the things we need to do to be successful in our role as a sales person.

A simple plan

More often than not, the best plans are the simplest. You don't need to use critical path software or fancy terms like "drivers of change," "change management" and "critical stakeholder objectives," etc.

A plan should be simple and to the point. It has two parts, (remember it's nothing more than an organized "to do" list).

The two components identify:

1. What you need to do.
2. When you're going to do it.

What needs to be done?

First up, write down a list – in bullet point form – of the things you need to do to be successful in your role. These points will vary from employer to employer, depending on your particular role. For example, some required tasks may be:

- Understand all product capabilities.
- Know possible benefits of each function or capability of your products.
- Lead generation activity via cold-calling and telemarketing.
- Improve product demonstration / presentation skills.
- Attend sales meetings / sales training.
- Prepare customer proposals.

- Visit current customers.
- Check that all potential customers are followed up.
- Qualify potential customers on sales forecast list.

Once you have a list of your main tasks, break each one down into the few steps that need to be done to ensure the task is completed.

For example:

Task 1:   Understand all product capabilities.
Action: 1. Read and understand all terms in product brochures.
            2. Read web site.
            3. Read sales guide.
            4. Trial and test product.
Task 2:   Improve product demonstration / presentation skills.
Action: 1. List generic features / benefits of products that should be shown.
            2. Write list in logical demonstration order.
            3. Arrange to watch a more experienced sales person do a product demonstration.
            4. Practice / rehearse demonstration to self.
            5. Practice / rehearse demonstration to colleagues.
Task 3:   Lead generation – conduct 30 cold calls a week
Action: 1. Cold-call companies on either side of each appointment.
            2. Keep a 2 hour appointment-free period each week for cold-calling.

When are you going to do it?

For each action, nominate a completion time.

Be sure to stagger the action dates so you're able to complete what it is you set out to do.

Objective	Action	Start Date	End Date	Completed Y/N
1. Use customer written references more in sales presentations	1. Call on customers 2. Request 1 written reference per week 3. Insert references into electronic presenter	1 Jun	30 Dec	
2. Obtain and review five competitor proposals	1. Ask for competitor proposals when each order is received	1 Jun	30 Dec	
3. Learn new products recently released	1. Read sales guide 2. Read Internet information 3. Read 3rd party esting report 4. Read user manual 5. Compare to competitor's equivalent products	1 Jun	30 Jun	
4. Review sales database for new business opportunities	1. Set a side 30 minutes each week	1 Jul	30 Aug	
5. Check entire sales territory is covered	1. Set a side1 hour per week 2. Scout sales territory for missed opportunities	1 Aug	30 Dec	

Note: If your entire plan can't be printed on two pages it's way too complicated.

Sales people new to this process should commence with only three tasks (objectives). More objectives can be added once the process becomes familiar, but to initially attempt to achieve more than three objectives will likely lead to failure.

Follow your road map

Now we have a plan, a road map of all the tasks we need to do in order to stay on track and succeed. Follow the plan and respect the time you've invested in thinking about what needs to be done.

On face value, this example may seem too simple. More experienced sales people may have more – and more complex – tasks on their "to do" list. For example, they may plan to improve their proposal template, or learn about a competitor's product in greater depth to establish its shortfalls.

Regardless of the level you're at, be sure to always work to improve your weaknesses first. Don't ignore them!

By achieving each small action you'll be surprised how easily you can achieve larger and multiple goals, almost without realizing it.

Review your plan quickly each week to ensure that you're on track and that you're adhering to the start and end dates you've assigned yourself to complete each action step. Revise and update your plan every two to three months, in line with your personal preference.

To complete all of your tasks your final step is to organize your time so you can achieve multiple tasks. We'll acknowledge this in the following chapter.

6.2

Our greatest competitor

If I only had a few more hours...

Sound familiar? The wish for more hours in the day to complete what needs to be done is a common desire.

But you won't get a few more hours in your day; it's not going to happen. What this means is that you're the one who must change – the number of hours in each day is not about to change.

Effective time management is a critical factor in determining your long term success in the world of sales. In fact it could be said that your greatest competitor is not a person or a company. With so much opportunity and so much to do, our greatest competitor is really time.

When you're generating leads through cold-calling you often find customers who recently bought a new product like yours from a competitor. This might have been six months ago, a week ago or even a day ago. If only you'd put yourself in front of the customer sooner you wouldn't have missed that opportunity. The difference between a sale and no sale was "time".

In your role as a sales person you should always stop and ask yourself, "Is what I'm doing right now going to make me money?" This self-checking mechanism will ensure your time is not wasted on trivial activities.

In fact, you need to become almost mercenary with your time. Your job is to sell. Anything that gets in your way should be eliminated from your schedule. Don't do other people's jobs for them as your job is too critical to the company's success.

We all agree you don't have enough time, so eliminate all else that is not core to you achieving your sales goals. Only do what is critically important for you to do; you simply don't have time to do anything else given the scale of opportunity out there.

Your success will come from being in the field speaking to as many customers as possible for as many of the available working hours as you can. Do all administration components of your role outside normal business hours and use normal business hours to maximize the available time to work in the field. Be generating leads or talking, in person, with customers, i.e. be where it matters.

The best sales people are rarely seen hanging around the sales office unless they have a phone to their ear and they're talking to a customer. There's little value in hanging around the office as the chances are you'll not be able to sell any products there.

In order to complete all your planned objectives and tasks you need to organize your time. Consider a typical week and create a timetable to help you see when you'll devote your attention to particular tasks. As we've shown here, be sure to acknowledge your personal circumstances and commitments too.

	MON	TUES	WED	THURS	FRI	SAT	SUN
6:00 a.m.		Exercise		Exercise		Exercise	Family Time
7:00 a.m.					Demonstration Rehearsal	↓	
8:00 a.m.	Review Prospects		Take Kids to School			Industry Reading	
9:00 a.m.		Telemarket		Cold Calling		Family Time	
10:00 a.m.							
11:00 a.m.					Appointments		
12:00 a.m.			Appointments				
1:00 a.m.	Appointments						
2:00 a.m.		Appointments					
3:00 a.m.				Appointments			
4:00 a.m.					Team Sales Meeting		
5:00 a.m.			Review Database for Opportunities				
6:00 a.m.							
7:00 a.m.						↓	↓

When booking an appointment, have respect for your customer's schedule, but also have respect for your own. Plan appointment times so they are geographically close to one another and avoid wasting time by extended travel between appointments. Make appointments within the constraints you've outlined in your generic weekly timetable.

Time is by far the scarcest resource you have. Respect it and use it to your advantage.

Quick recap: Action time

Your action plan

With so many demands on your time you need a simple plan to keep you on course and ensure that you don't get distracted or miss opportunities.

Your plan is basically an organized "to do" list, covering what you need to do and when you're going to do it.

If your plan can't be printed on two pages it's way too complicated.

Regardless of the level of sales proficiency you have, always work to improve your weaknesses first.

By achieving each small action you'll be surprised how easily you can achieve larger and multiple goals.

Your plan should be revised and updated every two to three months, in line with your personal preference.

Your success

Effective time management is a critical factor in determining your long term success in the world of sales.

Your success will come from being in the field speaking to as many customers as possible for as many of the available working hours as you can.

Your greatest competitor is not a person or a company, it's time.

With so much opportunity and so much to do you need to be mercenary about your time.

Your job is to sell. Anything that gets in your way should be eliminated from your schedule.

Stories from the frontline

The World Sales Championship

After a year of world-wide qualifying tournaments, where sales competitors earned the right to represent their zone, the week-long sudden death knockout round at the Sales Stadium was a fierce and brutal competition. The focus was now on the final two contestants competing for the winner's prize and the opportunity to be recognized as the year's World Sales Champion.

The stage was set, a brightly-lit glass walled office had been constructed in the center of the circular auditorium and 8 000 people were gathered there, waiting in darkness. They were there to watch the grand final appointments. As was tradition, the two contestants had not yet met and remained in separate backstage rooms while the master judge set the scene and explained the rules for the grand final appointments.

The rules

"Each sales professional will be given a sales folder which contains hard-copy sales support documents, product information and a USB flash drive containing an electronic presentation. The folders will be provided to the sales professionals fifteen minutes before their scheduled appointment time. Each sales professional can choose to use or disregard any of the details they have been provided."

Of keen interest to the audience was the product type, as this often determined the degree of difficulty it would present for the competitors.

"Tonight's product to be sold..." The audience was silent in anticipation. The judge paused for emphasis and extra effect. "...is a pallet containing 450 square brown cardboard boxes."

The audience was momentarily silent, waiting for additional information about the product. Eventually they realized the judge had said all he was going to say about the product and they laughed, as it was potentially the most difficult product imaginable. A brown cardboard box didn't provide the sales professionals with much to build a sales argument. This was clearly one product where all roads would lead to price being the only product differential.

"The cost of the product is $300, including taxes and delivery to the customer's premises. The goods cannot be sold for lower than this amount. The winner of the competition will be the contestant who sells their product for the highest dollar value in an honest and ethical manner. The judging panel will adjudicate on the ethics of the presentation and make a disqualification if required."

"In the true spirit of competitive professional selling, the winning contestant will receive the full prize money of $ 2 million and the runner up will receive nothing. Each appointment will be concluded once the order is signed by the customer, or when 20 minutes has elapsed, whichever occurs first. To minimize the chance of a draw and to increase intensity in this year's grand final appointments, we have altered two things."

The crowd was now completely intrigued. "Firstly, actors will not be engaged to represent customers. Instead, we will have actual business people as our customers. Both of our potential customers currently purchase cardboard boxes as part of their business. The second amendment to our usual format is an added incentive for the customers to negotiate strongly. The customer who purchases their product for the lowest price will receive prize money of $1 million."

The crowd clapped excitedly in appreciation of the new twists to the competition.

"The sales professionals will not be told anything about their customer prior to the appointment and they will not be advised about the customer's financial incentive to complete a purchase."

The customers

No two customers are ever the same. Some are easier to sell to than others. In the competition, as in the real world, it was considered the luck of the draw as to whether you received an easy or difficult customer to sell to. So it stood to reason that one sales professional would be at an advantage, depending on which customer they received in the draw.

The customers were then introduced to the audience and the main judge provided brief backgrounds.

Miss Emily was in her mid-thirties and appeared very corporate and polished in her presentation. She was President of her father's natural drug company, a business with significant market share across the four states they distributed to.

During college, Miss Emily spent her summer vacations in the purchasing department where she often negotiated purchases. She was also familiar with selling as her father insisted that she spend 4 years selling to customers before he permitted her to run the company. She was clearly experienced and a concern for any sales professional.

Mr. Chan, an older gentleman, was introduced as the owner-operator of a fresh fruit and vegetable supply company which operated 8 retail outlets across the largest state in the country. His company's turnover was similar to that of Miss Emily's company.

Mr. Chan was described as hard-working and a business owner that did not suffer fools easily. His success was derived from working long hours for many years. He was more casual in appearance than Miss Emily and was either nervous in this environment, or simply wasn't a person who enjoyed smiling.

The consensus

The audience muttered amongst themselves, discussing which customer would be easier to sell to. Most people seemed to feel that Miss Emily was the most preferred customer to draw. She would not be a pushover, but there seemed more personality to work with and she appeared more relaxed in this environment than did Mr. Chan.

It was thought that the difficulty in selling to Mr. Chan was not his curt nature, but the fact that he had built his business from the ground up. It was assumed that he understood the value of money and how vital cash flow is in a growing business. Mr. Chan would see any company expenditure as someone taking money directly out of his own pocket.

Miss Emily had a higher probability of taking her industry's higher profit margins for granted and there was a greater chance that her buying decision would be seen as spending company money, not her own.

The consensus was that Miss Emily would negotiate to what she thought would be a fair price but Mr. Chan would not stop until the price seemed more than fair in his favor.

The finalists

The customers left the stage and the final two sales professionals were brought out to meet each other for the first time. Jane and Billy Bob entered the stage from opposite directions.

Billy Bob was classically tall, dark and handsome. He wore his black three-piece suit with confidence. He appeared to have it all.

Jane appeared to challenge all expectations of what a typically successful sales person looks like. For starters, she wore a floral dress which was complimented with a bold and bright red handbag. She didn't even carry a briefcase. Her bright red high-heel shoes, which perfectly matched her lipstick and handbag, attracted the eye of everyone seated. Her smile was wide and as natural as could be.

Jane was one step beyond confident in her manner. Instantaneously she conveyed a friendly, comforting familiarity with her smile, dancing eyes and body language. Jane was the type of person who called anyone she ever met "sweetie" and did so without ever offending anyone. She silenced the audience as she walked across the stage.

Jane selected her customer's name at random from the hat offered by the main judge. Jane was to sell to Miss Emily and Billy Bob was to sell to Mr. Chan. A coin was tossed and it was decided that Jane would present first. The audience clapped politely as the contestants returned to read their sales folders and to wait back stage for their turn to meet with their potential customer.

The UK sales people had made a few friendly wagers on the result with their French counterparts who sat next to them in the stand. They had placed bets on the winning sale price, but no one had been willing to bet that the winning sale price would be greater than $ 380, given the product type and the customers involved.

Now that they'd seen Jane, no one was willing to bet that Billy Bob had any chance of winning.

The first contest: Jane and Miss Emily

Jane entered the office to meet Miss Emily, shook hands and sat down. Then, with her non-threatening country accent, she started by saying:

"Thank you so much for seeing me, how can we help?"

What followed could only be described as "sales poetry." Jane asked question after question in an inquisitive yet sincere manner. The conversation ebbed and flowed with Miss Emily doing most of the talking and Jane effortlessly prompting her and guiding the discussion. Those watching this dialogue easily forgot that a competition was taking place. It seemed like the two women were about to leave the office and go to the nearest cafe for a coffee and a more involved chat.

Jane had created an atmosphere where Miss Emily was discussing her situation and experiences without realizing the hidden meaning this held for Jane. She established that:

1. Miss Emily's company had grown 20% in the past 12 months, despite the economic downturn. Her products experienced greater demand in hard times.
2. The company was looking for a second warehouse as they were running out of storage area in their existing warehouse.
3. They were having issues with quality and continuity of supply with their current cardboard box supplier and were using a broker who imported them from the Far East.
4. Their current supplier had made extensive promises but failed to live up to them.
5. One particular box size was the one used for all the company's products. Each box carried 48 bottles of product to their retailers.

Jane was able to get Miss Emily talking about her role and the challenges she faced as the boss's daughter in charge of longer serving employees. Less than 10 minutes had passed when Jane stopped asking questions and said:

"About these boxes we can help you with, I don't want to automatically assume that you're keen to change to us as your new supplier, solely based on our reputation. Do you mind if I take a few minutes to give you an idea of how we do things? I would love you to appreciate why our customers enjoy working with us."

Miss Emily happily agreed and Jane continued as she opened her sales folder to retrieve the flash drive. "I understand from your perspective they are just cardboard boxes, so I'll be brief, but we do take them seriously and are proud of what we do," she added.

Without fuss, Jane loaded the Flash drive into the provided laptop and quickly displayed the image on the large flat-screen TV in the office.

"I would like to show you ten pictures so you can see why we're passionate about what we do." Jane stood up and enthusiastically walked about the office as she discussed each image.

Jane's images depicted their production factory and premises. It told the story of the entire operation, from raw material supply through to product dispatch, invoicing and even the accounting department. She made various "off the cuff" comments as she progressed through each photograph. Most of the images featured employees doing their job and Jane made a few remarks like, "Oh these are some of the people your support will help." Another time she quickly said, "some more local jobs."

Jane paused on a close-up of a completed box moving down the production line. She passionately explained different technical aspects of the box, pointing to the parts that she was talking about. She explained why the box was corrugated the way it was, how it folded and why it was joined together in a certain way and why it had greater strength than other "average" boxes.

Miss Emily had never thought about or heard someone describe a cardboard box in such detail before. Jane's passionate points made for interesting listening. She made a further, brief comment that the box in the photo was in fact the same size as the one they would supply to Miss Emily. She said that they were particularly proud of this one as it was their most popular. And they had worked hard to get production costs down on this size to such an extent that they could now dispatch it to their large national customers for as low as $1.17 a piece on high volume orders. It was a brief comment, almost a throwaway line.

Jane's energy and enthusiasm was intoxicating, to such an extent that Miss Emily, not to mention the 8 000 members of the audience, were now "buying" cardboard boxes in their mind.

A palatable price point

Jane asked if Miss Emily had any questions about what she had just been shown and if it had all made sense. As she was sitting back down at the desk and opening her folder Jane said, "I hope I didn't tell you too much and bore you?" She smiled at Miss Emily in a way that discouraged an answer. Jane continued on, "Right, let's see if our price points are low enough for your type of business."

Jane was patiently flicking through the pages of her sales folder as if she was looking for the price list. As she was looking she asked, "Miss Emily may I ask, based on what you've seen today, are you happy to work with us and let us help you with your cardboard boxes?" Miss Emily conceded that she was happy with what she had seen. So Jane asked, "Setting price aside for a moment, are you happy to use us as your supplier for all your cardboard box requirements?"

Miss Emily agreed that this would be the case, based on acceptable pricing. "Will you be sharing your business with more than one supplier, or will you be using us exclusively on this line?" asked Jane. "Yes, I'm happy to use you exclusively if the price is right," responded Miss Emily. "OK, then I will structure my prices on your annual requirements and automatically apply our high volume discounts to the price instead of our single pallet rate," said Jane. She was so smooth in her delivery that Miss Emily didn't realize the hidden meaning in this.

Miss Emily wouldn't be able to creditably ask for a discount, based on the volume she was to buy, as Jane had cleverly removed it as a justification to ask for a discount. Jane then found the price list page and looked as if she was taking time to ensure that she was quoting the right size box. She slowly said, "OK, our volume sales price with cash terms is twelve thirty dollars per thousand pieces ex-factory."

Jane had been looking down at her folder as she started to read the price out but at the moment she delivered it she was watching Miss Emily's immediate reaction. Miss Emily was a little stuck for a moment as she could not make sense of the price. She asked what it worked out to be. "$1.23 a piece," Jane replied without adding anything further.

Jane sat and waited for Miss Emily to catch up; she didn't talk or feel inclined to fill in the silence in any way.

Miss Emily eventually asked, "Well, that is a little extreme isn't it?"

"Why do you say that?" Jane calmly inquired. She didn't have a good answer ready and needed more time to think.

"Is that after discount?" Miss Emily asked.

Jane looked down at her price book as if she was checking and said, "Yes, it's our discounted rate, I have quoted the high volume rate and the cash terms rate."

"Cash terms ... well, what are your cash terms?" asked Miss Emily.

"Full payment via direct deposit into our bank account within three working days from delivery," explained Jane.

"But we work on a month-end account basis, we don't want to operate on cash terms," said Miss Emily.

"Oh" said Jane as she thought for a brief moment. "Well, if we're able to apply our cash term prices for you and operate on a month-end account would you be happy to proceed with us?"

Miss Emily was gaining confidence. "Well no, I am a little shocked by the price. To be honest it's very expensive!"

"Oh, really?" asked Jane, "Compared to what?"

Again, Jane just waited for Miss Emily to respond. Miss Emily was stuck, as obviously she didn't have other quotes to relate to. So she could only talk about what they were currently paying.

"Compared to what we currently pay!" Miss Emily responded.

"Which is?" prompted Jane.

"Under a dollar a piece," Miss Emily proudly announced.

Jane sought to clarify, "Is that 99 cents? Or 50 cents? Or..."

"94 cents a piece," confessed Miss Emily.

Jane remained calm and friendly. She had not changed in her disposition since the presentation began.

She asked, "OK, so you currently pay 94 cents. Does that include tax?"

"No," said Miss Emily.

"Does it include delivery?"

"Yes it does," Miss Emily clarified.

"And the payment terms that apply for that price?" Jane asked.

"Well we do pay that invoice on cash terms because it is related to the sea container delivery."

Jane looked puzzled but said nothing. Miss Emily saw that she needed to clarify.

"Well, because when we receive them from our broker we have to take delivery of a full sea container and make payment upon receipt. It's the only supplier that we do not operate a month-end account with."

Jane thought she now understood the situation and sought to clarify. "How many pallets do you need to pay for at a time?" she asked.

"From memory, I think there are 44 pallets in a sea container," said Miss Emily.

Boxed into a corner

Jane summarized her understanding. "So you have to buy a full sea container each time, containing 44 pallets of boxes. You take delivery of 44 pallets at a time, pay for them and store them all in your warehouse until you need them, and they cost you 94 cents plus tax a piece."

Miss Emily confirmed this was the situation.

"So you're currently paying 94 cents and we're at $1.23."

Jane took a calculator out of her handbag. Not surprisingly, the calculator was an unusual bright red color. Miss Emily could not help but notice and comment on it. The observation helped ease some of the tension that was starting to build.

Jane did the calculation in front of Miss Emily so that she could see the calculator screen. (1.23 minus 0.94 = 0.29)

"So there's a 29 cent differential between us and your current expenditure."

Miss Emily agreed, albeit hesitantly since they were now talking about cents.

"I think you said there are 48 bottles in each box of your product," Jane said as she slowly punched in the next calculation, allowing Miss Emily to follow what was happening (0.29 / 48 units = 0.00604).

"So to change to us it would incur an additional cost of less than a cent per bottle. Can your wholesale price sustain a one cent price adjustment?" asked Jane.

Miss Emily paused for thought, as quite obviously, the wholesale price could increase by this small amount. She had previously told Jane how strong their recent sales growth had been, so there was no logic in not agreeing to a mere point six of a cent change in the wholesale unit price of her product. Miss Emily was clearly thinking about Jane's point and was trying hard to come up with a logical reason as to why she didn't want to pay more for her boxes.

In the end Miss Emily said, "I need more discount, it's not going to work for us at your price points."

"Alright then, let's put money aside for a moment," said Jane, calmly and amicably. "Who would you prefer to deal with if both our prices were exactly the same?"

"You" said Miss Emily without hesitation.

"May I ask why?" Jane politely inquired.

"Well, I do understand the quality of your product and it would be easier for us to deal with someone local," said Miss Emily, not being conscious of the fact that Jane should be providing the sales arguments, not her.

Jane continued, "So given the reliability of our superior quality, and the "lack of head aches" we represent, by dealing with us locally, compared to your experience with your current supplier, are we worth the small premium of 29 cents a piece?"

Jane left her comments at that. Miss Emily decided to be honest with Jane but she wasn't going to give up just yet.

"Jane yes, you're right. You are worth it, but we haven't allowed for the higher expenditure in our budget and cost structure."

Jane responded sincerely and without fuss, but more slowly than before.

"OK that's fair enough, I was hoping we would be able to help you. It's difficult for us to do business at overseas labor price points and we're not about compromising the quality of our product or service. Our reputation is too important to us. I guess, from our perspective we don't see our business as just selling cardboard boxes. Our customers deal with us for a number of reasons. Mostly it's because they consider the full cost of doing business elsewhere, as opposed to dealing with us.

Firstly, dealing locally protects and creates local jobs. We understand that this isn't a great motivator in a business decision, but the last thing you want is a TV crew knocking on your door asking you why child labor is being used to make your boxes. Our reliability of delivery prevents you incurring other hidden costs like the costs of not being able to dispatch your orders because your boxes have not arrived. We prevent the cost of having your products roll around the back of a delivery truck because of the high quality standards that we manufacturer to. You can buy your boxes from us, as and when you require them. You can even buy in pallet lot amounts. This helps your cash flow and saves you interest costs on your bank overdraft. There's no need to buy 44 pallets at a time when you deal with us. We'll save you warehouse space, in your case, about 40 pallet bays in your warehouse. With a saving like that you may not need to buy a secondary warehouse. If this is the case, how much will you save then?"

Miss Emily had not considered the warehouse space-saving in her assessment of the costs. She thought hard as to what could be a further justification for asking for a discount but Jane had covered payment terms and had already given the high volume selling rate. She had nowhere to go.

As Jane was closing her sales folder and pushing her chair back as if preparing to leave, she said, "Oh that's a shame sweetie, I was really hoping to be able to work with you."

Last chance
Miss Emily was starting to get the idea that not only was Jane not prepared to move, but she may not have been able to move on price. It appeared as if she had reached her bottom line and was walking away from a potential sale. Miss Emily understood from Jane's presentation that the National Rate was $1.17, so perhaps her price was as good as it was going to get.

Miss Emily said, "Jane, I appreciate your position, and to be honest I would like to work with you too, but if we're to move ahead we need your product to be cheaper."

Jane took a moment to look at Miss Emily and thought about this comment. She reached for her sales folder again and took out her calculator, while turning to the price list. She punched in some numbers and said. "As a show of good faith, if we discount by a further 5% from the ex-factory price that we discussed, will you place the order?" Jane looked at her calculator and said, "That makes it one point one, six, eight, five which is just under $1.17 a piece, ex-factory."

Miss Emily agreed and Jane wrote up the order for the pallet of goods. Jane included a $ 17 pallet delivery charge. She stepped Miss Emily through the written order, outlining the costs, pointing at the figures with her pen as she read them out. When she got to the delivery fee Jane said, "It costs us $17 to deliver the pallet and that is our national rate for delivery which we pass on to all customers. Unfortunately we can't do anything about that, as it's a real and direct cost."

Miss Emily signed the order and the audience applauded.

Jane had made the sale at a total value of $ 542.82, a price few would have thought she could have achieved in the circumstances. When interviewed by the judge after the appointment, Miss Emily said she accepted the price because she thought that Jane started close to the bottom line. She didn't perceive that there was a valid chance to go lower; it was obvious that it was a higher quality cardboard box so she assumed the production costs were relatively high.

The second contest: Billy Bob and Mr. Chan

Billy Bob walked in and introduced himself. He took a seat after Mr. Chan invited him to do so. Initially intimidated with the coldness of Mr. Chan's body language and facial expression, Billy Bob started to gain confidence after shaking hands with Mr. Chan. Experience told him that based on his handshake, he was a fair person. Mr. Chan's handshake was neither limp nor overly strong and this gave Billy Bob encouragement.

Billy Bob started by saying, "I like your office" and followed it with a slight grin. Mr. Chan replied with an equally dry comment, "Yes it is very plush, I paid for it with all the discounts I receive from my suppliers."

Billy Bob started with all sorts of questions but he quickly discovered that Mr. Chan was quite deliberately giving him one-word answers.

In preparation for the appointment, Billy Bob had practiced using the electronic presentation and spent some time playing with numbers. He assumed that given that it was the final, the sales price would have to have a healthy sales margin if there was going to be any chance of winning.

Billy Bob had worked numbers and felt that a minimum pallet sell price of $ 540, after any discount, would be needed to have a chance of winning. In order to be able to strike a deal with the customer, he calculated that if he discussed a selling price of $ 1.35 a piece then, if he needed, he could give away 50 boxes on the pallet as an incentive. This implied that 400 boxes at a piece price of $ 1.35 would bring a sale price of $ 540 for the whole pallet and this was approximately where the price had to land.

He spent most of his time understanding the attributes and technical benefits of the cardboard box, as it was a high quality product with a special new coating, making it stronger than most other cardboard boxes.

Mr. Chan's one-word answers were not rude, and they may well have been completely honest, but they weren't giving Billy Bob a chance to fact find.

"From your perspective Mr. Chan, may I ask how important quality is for you in this decision?" Billy Bob asked.

"It isn't," Mr. Chan advised.

"Why is that?" asked Billy Bob.

"It's a disposable product with a short lifespan, so there is no point in me paying for a premium product, it would be a waste of money."

Boxing with shadows

Billy Bob established that Mr. Chan used the boxes to transport his product to each of his retail stores. He would use the box two to three times before replacing it. He also established that he didn't believe in organic fruit and vegetables because customers refused to pay a premium price for them.

Billy Bob decided to abandon his intended sales presentation and change tack. He felt that Mr. Chan would not appreciate an electronic presentation and he got the distinct feeling that it didn't matter what he said about his company, product or solution, Mr. Chan would just come back to price. If this were the "real" world, Billy Bob would have left this potential customer behind for his competitors to pursue. Mr. Chan was that one-in-a-hundred that could only see price and nothing else. Billy Bob continued on.

"Mr. Chan I have a wonderful sales presentation which helps me tell you how I have the best cardboard box in the entire world. But I kind of suspect that you don't really care about all the sales fluff."

Mr. Chan smiled and Billy Bob knew he was finally starting to converse with his customer in a common language.

Billy Bob continued, "If you like, I have some really good stuff about how environmentally-friendly we are as a corporate partner, how we recycle and care for the planet, the whole bit. If you want we can take a few minutes and hug a tree together."

Mr. Chan just smiled and shook his head from side to side, but he did appreciate Billy Bob's dry humor.

"So you care about..." Billy Bob prompted.

"Price," said Mr. Chan, but this time he wasn't smiling.

"So, forget all the sales justification, you just want to buy a box!" Billy Bob stated for clarification and to attempt, one last time, to find something that mattered to his potential customer.

"No," said Mr. Chan.

Billy Bob looked at Mr. Chan in a way that asked for further explanation.

"I don't just want to buy a box, I want to buy a cheap box, a very cheap box," said Mr. Chan, emphasizing a point that had long been made.

"Well Mr. Chan, you've come to the right place for that." Billy Bob declared. He got out his price book and asked, "Mr. Chan, are you in a position to change your supplier to our company, if we're in a position to help you?"

Mr. Chan just nodded and said, "If the price is right."

"What price do you need?" Billy Bob asked.

Mr. Chan said, "Nice try, junior," to which Billy Bob replied, "Well it's my job, I have to ask these questions."

Think outside the box

Billy Bob was sitting with his chair pulled up to Mr. Chan's desk and, as he flicked through the pages of his folder, he paused at a particular image and looked up at Mr. Chan. He said, "Why are you buying cardboard boxes?" Not wanting or waiting for an answer he continued, "It doesn't make sense does it? Why don't you use plastic crates or tubs? They'll cost you about 20 dollars each but you should get years out of each crate."

Mr. Chan was taken aback by Billy Bob's approach as it would do him out of a sale. It impressed Mr. Chan that Billy Bob was genuinely thinking about his best interests. Mr. Chan said, "Good idea Billy Bob, but we did consider that a few years ago and the plastic crate does not allow enough airflow for the fruit and vegetables. Also, I personally didn't like using them, because I thought cardboard protected the fruit better and the plastic was too hard should the fruit move during transport."

"Actually, what did you say that you pay for a box at the moment?" Billy Bob asked.

"I didn't," said Mr. Chan, quickly returning to curtness.

"I've got the strongest box," said Billy Bob excitedly.

"Look," he said, pointing to an image in his sales folder. "We coat our boxes differently and they are stronger and will last you longer. I probably can't compete on price on a box-for-box basis, given how we make them, but our lab reports have shown that they are tested to be twice as strong as our nearest competitor. Let's assume that our product lasts twice as long and because you reuse them you should get at least double the number of trips out of our boxes. We probably don't cost twice as much as you're currently paying, so we'll be cheaper for you."

"OK, let's work this out," Billy Bob continued, as he turned to his price page.

"There are lots of schemes and different ways of pricing our products with free cartons, loyalty points, with or without delivery fees, etc. I'm just going to cut to the bottom line so we can calculate if it's worthwhile buying from us, OK?"

Mr. Chan agreed and started to appear interested in where Billy Bob was going. "Delivered to you we can sell you a pallet of 450 boxes for, bottom line $ 539.87. This means a cost of $ 1.1997 a box. You said you get 2-3 trips from each box at the moment. Let's assume that we can deliver you 4-6 trips per box. Let's say on average, 5 trips. This means $1.1997 divided by five is an effective cost of 23.99 cents per box, per trip. So what do you pay at the moment?" Billy Bob asked, more assertively.

"94 cents," Mr. Chan conceded.

"Honestly?" asked Billy Bob.

Mr. Chan smiled and nodded sincerely.

"So, 94 cents divided by two and a half trips is 37 cents per box, per trip. Based on an assumption that you get five trips on average, we will be cheaper for you." Billy Bob was making sure that he beat Mr. Chan to any objection. "You may get more than five trips or you may get less, but it's worth the look," Billy Bob stated adamantly.

Mr. Chan thought Billy Bob's point was a valid one and a fair assessment. Billy Bob had been so smooth in his delivery that Mr. Chan didn't realize that his suggestion about plastic crates was Billy Bob deliberately building his story.

Mr. Chan looked at the price Billy Bob had mentioned because he had written it on a piece of paper straight away. $ 539.87 sounded like it was a well thought out price. It wasn't the typical sales talk of "round figures" like $ 500 or $ 550; it sounded as if it could be a real number and possibly the lowest he could go.

Mr. Chan said, "OK, I will buy it at your price if you guarantee that I will get at least 5 trips on average for each box."

Without hesitation Billy Bob said, "No we can't do that, I don't have a crystal ball. I can't guarantee anything. That's not business. I've done my part and given you our bottom line and a fair price, but it's only fair that in return you do your part and buy at least a pallet. That way you can trial it."

"But it is still a high price per box," argued Mr. Chan.

The deal breaker

Billy Bob pulled out a list from his sales folder and gave it to Mr. Chan. He said, "Here is a list of our competitors. Every one of them may sell you a lower-priced box. We can't, because of the quality we manufacture to. No-one on that list will match our quality, but I don't expect you to believe me or any other sales person you meet. But we can help you and we'll save you money if you buy one pallet to start with and see how we go."

Billy Bob then pulled 15 letters out of the back of his sales folder. As he fanned them out across Mr. Chan's desk, he said, "I don't want you to believe me, I'm a salesman, but I do know that we'll not disappoint you. These customers have taken the time to put in writing how they feel about us." Billy Bob continued to cover Mr. Chan's desk with client references, sitting them side-by-side.

Billy Bob was so fired up that everyone forgot it was all part of a competition. People in the stands were close to applauding the show Billy Bob was putting on. It was exceptional, his enthusiasm was truly infectious.

Mr. Chan said, "OK I will take the chance and buy the pallet at your price and I will take the risk that they may not last as long as you think. But I want something for taking that chance."

"Mr. Chan, I understood where you are at and I gave you our best shot. I can't go any lower than what I've quoted," said Billy Bob earnestly.

"It's a deal breaker then?" said Mr. Chan.

Billy Bob replied with "OK, I'll throw in 10 free boxes, but only on this first pallet."

"Thank you," said Mr. Chan, as he stood up to shake Billy Bob's hand.

The audience applauded at what was a fantastic effort under the circumstances. Billy Bob had achieved a total sale price of $ 527.88, not even 3% less than where he'd set his sights.

And the winner is...

Jane won the first prize of $2 million. Her sale price was only $14.94 greater than Billy Bob's. Charging for delivery had made all the difference.

The two performances surpassed all audience expectations. Few had thought that selling a cardboard box could have been such a passionate affair and so cleverly negotiated.

Final recap

By not presenting yourself as the typical sales person, the door is left wide open for you to succeed against your competitors.

When you understand the power of making sales presentations with confidence, integrity and tenacity, you'll quickly see that there is an enormous amount of opportunity.

By respecting the steps of the sale you'll overcome hurdles you previously thought restrictive, such as limited market share, limited product range, or low brand awareness.

Selling to referrals and customers with whom you have a relationship is appealing, but this shouldn't limit your sales success; you can approach the wider, available market proactively.

Naturally, you can't do everything we've discussed in this book on each sales call, but have the confidence to use the tools and techniques as and when you require them.

Remember that providing goods and services without obtaining profit and an appropriate financial return is charity. It's not selling.

For optimal results in your sales career:

- Have a positive attitude.
- Exercise a good work ethic.
- Don't wait for the world to come to you.
- Never give in.

- Be diligent and be thorough.
- Assume nothing.
- Keep thinking about what you're doing.
- Care.
- Don't waste time.
- Ignore trivial, negative discussions.
- Believe that you are the difference.
- Believe that you can be better.
- Believe in yourself.

In selling you never get to the finish line. You may have performed better this month than last month. You may have performed better this year than last year. You might be better at your job this week than last week. That's OK. Always look to be better, never look to be finished.

We wish you luck as you sell more products, more profitably, more often.

Enjoy success!

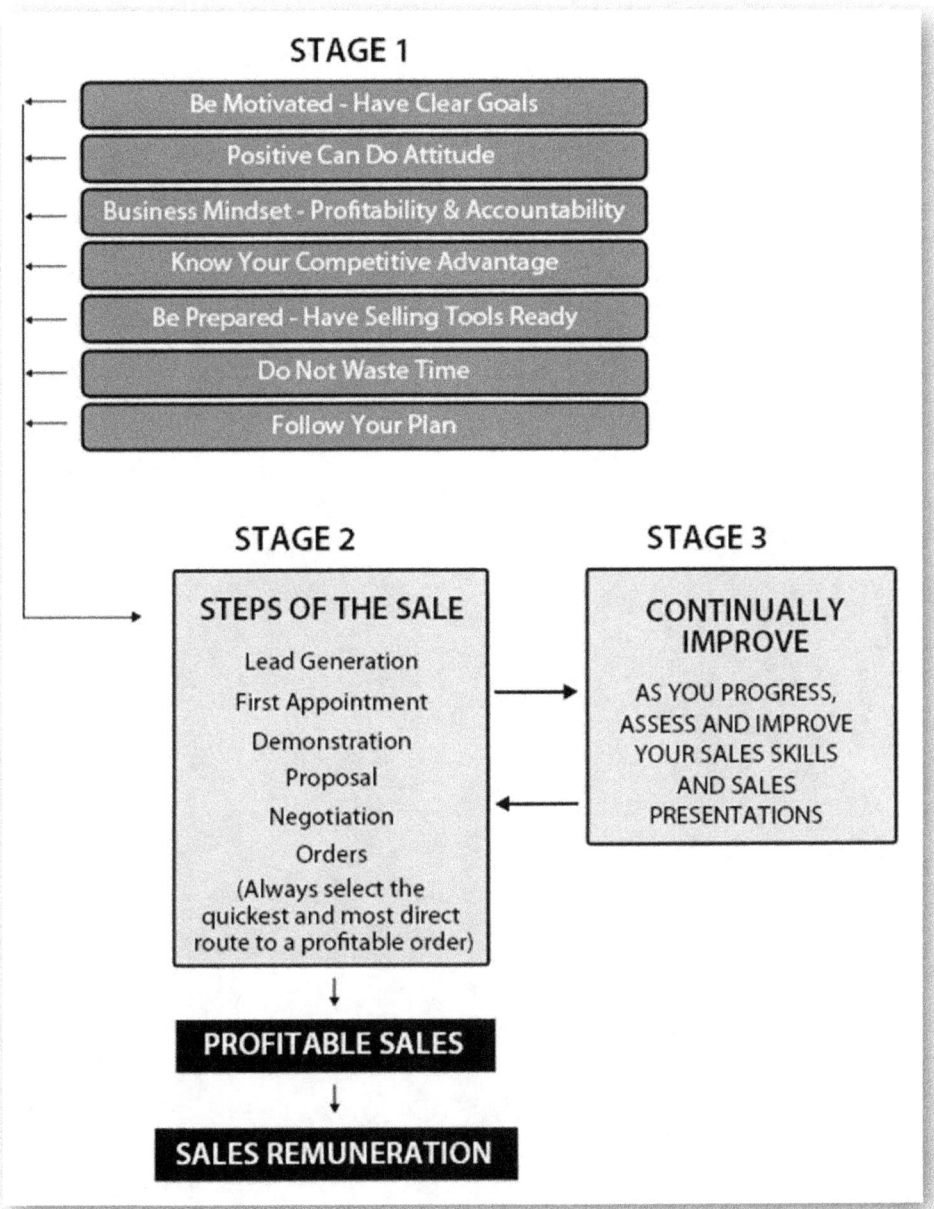